CREATIVE
DRAMA
IN GROUPWORK

Sue Jennings

WINSLOW

Telford Road • Bicester
Oxon OX6 0TS • UK
Telephone: 01869 244644
Facsimile: 01869 320040

Dedication

This book is dedicated with much love to my mother Alice Edna Jennings, a dancer and counsellor, who is a very creative person herself.

First published in 1986 by
Winslow Press Ltd,
Telford Road, Bicester, Oxon OX6 0TS
Reprinted 1987, 1988, 1989, 1990,
1991, 1992, 1993, 1994, 1995, 1996, 1997

ISBN 0 86388 050 9

002-0162/PRINTED IN GREAT BRITAIN (HtP)

Contents

Acknowledgements

I have many people to thank for stimulation, support and sources during the preparation of this book. At the beginning I must thank my secretary, Margaret Davis, and Gill Darvill for their constant attention and contributions to this manuscript.

My family, Andy & Jaqui, Ros, Hal and also the boys are a continuing source of creative stimulus to me in my work and are very tolerant of my preoccupation. I must thank my colleagues at Hertfordshire College of Art and Design, especially John Evans and Phil Jones; David Powley from St. Johns College York; and also my colleagues and students from Greece, Norway and USA, in particular Yiorgos Polos, Ase Minde and Robert Landy. I shall always be in their debt.

My dramatherapy students at St. Albans and York for the last decade (1976-1986) have been a constant challenge and resource for my work. A very special thank you to them. My clients in various hospitals (both in UK and overseas), in social services and probation, and also in my private practice have taught me most of what I know.

I must give a special tribute to Fr. Harold Beech, Dr. Murray Cox, Eric Steadman and dear friend and colleague, Alida Gersie for support and sustenance at times of creative darkness.

Preface

Drama for All

Although many readers will be working in clinical settings such as hospitals, others will be involved in the increasing use of community rather than institutional care. There will also be those who work in the educational field. In all of these areas the working climate has been undergoing rapid and often drastic change. Both personnel and equipment are more scarce; and professionals must function as best they can in the context of limited resources.

This book reflects such changes and does not assume that resources are limitless. It is an optimistic book in that it aims to make things possible.

Drama can help all of us, if we choose to explore its potential. For example, it may enable us to acquire the clarity and conviction which we need in the debating group, the administration meeting or with management. It is intended that this book should reduce the historical gulf between 'us' and 'them', between the givers and the receivers, by acknowledging the potential in drama for ourselves and our staff groups as well as for our clients.

A book is no substitute for experience, particularly in a dynamic medium such as creative drama. Therefore, the reader is urged to take courage and experiment, to seek advice (and, of course, training), and to learn by 'reflective action'. It is *not* advisable simply to use these pages as a working manual.

How to use this book

Part I of this book should be read in its entirety before selecting material from Part II. What has been attempted is to provide pointers, to draw attention to issues which may not yet have been addressed, to share some of the author's considerable accumulated knowledge of the subject, and to stimulate the reader's own innate creativity. The guidelines given in the following chapters will encourage users to try things for themselves and take some risks, so that new ideas and techniques may emerge.

The exercises listed in Part II will undoubtedly provide the basis for many group sessions. However, group leaders should discuss and plan and generate their own variations on exercises and games. Above all, there is much to be gained from careful thought before each session, and by reflection during and after the event. Guidance on how to use the exercises in Part II can be found on page 31.

A word of encouragement

This book has been written because I believe that everybody is potentially creative, whether worker or client. Some of us have to discover or rediscover our own creativity; and some of us are tired or jaded. Others are daunted when faced with groups that are too large, with clients who are very disturbed or disabled, and with constantly diminishing resources.

Working with this book won't change your budget, however it could give you some new energy and sense of worth so that you go on fighting.

Remember that creativity is catching. If you can feel creative and spontaneous and above all, hopeful, your clients will also experience this.

Creative drama is an adventure and, like all adventures, has inherent risks and dangers. Nevertheless it can also be playful, enriching — and sometimes magic!

Go slay the dragon and bring back the treasures!

Sue Jennings

Introduction

A significant proportion of readers of this book will be professionals who are already familiar with running groups of various kinds. Others may have used drama-related activities such as role play with clients in their own field of work. There may also be those who would very much like to venture into the use of drama, but who have as yet lacked the courage to try it.

Many features of group work such as group dynamics are broadly similar, no matter what the setting; and it is not proposed to discuss general issues here. However, a creative drama group may differ in certain respects from other therapeutic or social skills groups; and it is the distinctive nature, scope and underlying philosophy of such work that will be considered in this opening chapter. Drama has been used for the purposes of healing, education, spiritual enlightenment and ritual for many centuries, both in the Western world (viz. early Greek theatre) and in other cultures such as Asia and Africa, where ritual still plays a most important role.

Therapy through the medium of drama began to take shape in the early 1960's, when mime, movement and improvisation were found to produce encouraging results with groups of mentally handicapped and mentally ill patients. The approaches adopted were so favourably received that nurses, therapists, psychologists, psychiatrists and social workers became increasingly interested in the potentialities of drama. In recent years, teachers have explored these areas with comparable success, for example, among poor achievers. Two distinct fields of work have now emerged, namely Remedial Drama and Dramatherapy, each generating new ideas and research. The rationale of this book and the ideas put forward derive from many years of practical experience in both these fields. The reader who is relatively unfamiliar with these activities may wish to refer to the Reading List supplied at the end of Part I. It is hoped that the increasing number of dramatherapists will also find value in this book. Although it is not written for a specific profession, emphasis is placed on *good practice* which should be the aim of any worker using creative drama with groups. Whilst the author would like to see trained dramatherapists working alongside other professionals in a whole range of settings, such an ideal situation is still relatively rare. Furthermore, the application of drama in groupwork spreads beyond the remit of a single profession. Many share the philosophy that 'doing' (ie. action) is an important way of bringing about change. Sadly, we tend to divide people into the doers and the thinkers. This book, however, is about doing *and* thinking, or 'reflective action'. It is intended to circumvent the professional boundaries of different disciplines and to refer to areas which are of common concern to all who work with people.

Why drama?

In the past, the use of drama in groupwork has either been considered too 'dangerous', and therefore to be avoided at all costs, or else it has been used as a Friday afternoon filler when nothing particular has been planned. A variation on the latter is the 'Drama is good for you' approach, in which such activities have been used almost as one might prescribe a daily dose of laxative. There exists some notion that drama will do you good but no-one stops to ask the question — Why? In the following sections there will be an opportunity to ask such questions in order to refine our practice and be selective in its applications.

Creative drama has benefitted a wide range of clients or user groups, including mentally or physically handicapped people, under achievers in schools, families in therapy and children and adults with a variety of social or clinical problems. It has also helped those with a problem such as a stammer when the treatment programme has incorporated role play and related activities. The exact nature of any group and the choice of exercises depends upon the age and type of client, and on the group's overall programme and objectives.

Empathy and security

Whatever the context or composition of the group, two factors will always apply. First, while training in this work increases confidence and improves the range of skills, a leader's attitude and ability to empathise are always of paramount importance. Second, a well run group has, by its very nature, great therapeutic potential: within it, members can find a sense of community, security and support. Here, they may explore, take risks, increase their understanding of self, build confidence and also make changes. Creative drama in a group setting can be a means of finding out about the unknown whilst, at the same time, having an equal value in reinforcing the known.

Sue Jennings

Dramatherapist and social anthropologist, Sue Jennings trained as a dancer and actress and performed professionally in the theatre before teaching and then innovating the application of drama as therapy. She was a founder member of the BritishAssociation for Dramatherapy, and held the first Research Fellowship in Dramatherapy at St John's College, York.

Until recently she was a senior lecturer and course leader in Dramatherapy and Social Anthropology at Hertfordshire College of Art and Design, St Albans.

Currently she is conducting research with abusing families in a social services department and working with infertility at a London teaching hospital.

She is consultant dramatherapist to Hertfordshire College of Art and Design and to the Arts and Therapy Centre, Athens.

Part I
The Scope & Possibilities of Creative Drama in Groupwork

Exploration of Structure and Roles in Group Drama

Structure

Social psychologists have observed that we organise our lives in a dramatic structure or framework. We can view ourselves and others in a series of scenes and episodes, some of which have a consciously predictable structure, such as the way we organise a celebration or a formal meeting. Such scenes have a conscious 'text' and usually the 'roles' are prescribed. Each scene has its 'key actors', a 'supporting cast', and a known ending.

There are other scenes which do not appear to be predictable — chance meetings; informal gatherings; daily interactions with the family. However, on examination we find that many of these scenes can have predictable elements including an unacknow-ledged 'sub-text', 'roles' which may be inflexible, and a seemingly inevitable ending.

During the course of certain creative drama exercises, formal and less formal structure of interaction can be explored by members of the group.

Roles

There is sometimes a reluctance to admit that we constantly engage in role playing. It is the word 'playing', perhaps, that makes us feel it is not *real?* Or is it that being in a role somehow implies that we are not being ourselves?

In fact, each one of us adopts a variety of roles; indeed, it is important to remember that we develop the capacity to role play from a very early age — about ten months. It is most significant that we become, as it were, 'mobile in character', even before we become 'mobile in body'. Our role play is further developed through play in childhood and through experimentation in adolescence, whilst also being shaped by the family and outside world. On reaching adulthood, each individual has embraced a variety of roles which together form our role repertoire, by means of which our external and internal worlds are related.

In creative drama groups, individuals may be found to have difficulty in making connections between these internal and external facets. Others may have developed rigid and fixed roles in early life; or else inappropriate roles have emerged, often through inadequate or faulty 'modelling'. Drama not only helps us come to terms with our everyday life and facilitates exploration of our inner life, but it also enables us to transcend ourselves and go beyond our everyday limits and boundaries.

Through various forms of dramatic structure and dramatic role play the group leader aims to achieve some of the following for group members:

▶ to *expand* the limits of our experience and stimulate our artistic and aesthetic sense

▶ to *uncover* the predictable structures that trap us in unhelpful behaviours and to find some creative alternatives

▶ to *re-develop* appropriate roles through practice and re-modelling until they become more natural and less conscious

▶ to *encourage* the extension of role repertoire, ie. a range of roles that are appropriate to different situations

▶ to *create* new possibilities for experiencing scenes in unusual or unprescribed ways

▶ to *discover* ways of connecting internalised responses with external behaviour, and vice versa.

The basic premise for the above section is that we all have potential for some change — of life, of love, of vision — given the opportunity and the right kind of support. One way in which to explore these possibilities is through drama, for which *everyone* has potential — although they may not be aware of it.

The Focus of Drama Work in Groups

Those who venture into drama work with groups naturally hope that their approach will produce creative results and encourage expression, whilst also perhaps bringing about new insights and enabling members to accomplish tasks. However, as described in 'Models of Practice in Dramatherapy' (Journal of Dramatherapy, Vol 7, No 1) a specific focus tends to emerge, largely determined by the type and needs of the group members. Three fairly distinct types of focus can be identified. These are described below, and form the basis for advice offered in later sections. Part II exercises have also been classified according to these categories although many of the activities can be used to achieve different objectives simply by presenting them in a different way, thus making them suitable for more than one of the following types of group.

Focus on Creativity and Expression

The emphasis in such a group is placed on the creative development and aesthetic experience of the participants. Drama activities can include movement, mime and improvisation; puppets and masks; and text and story work. Members may also be encouraged to focus on performance eg. the Christmas play or the Summer Pageant. Productions should avoid becoming competitive, but it is sometimes valuable for creative experiences to be shared with a wider audience.

Apart from giving creative and aesthetic enjoyment, a group of this nature provides stimulation, encouragement and a heightened experience of self. The work also increases an individual's confidence through development of the imagination and the tapping of undiscovered potential. Furthermore, it improves communication and encourages co-operation (an important social skill), for members have to work together to create an improvisation or production. The leader's role as facilitator is most important: a balance has to be struck between allowing the group's creative energies to meander without any sort of direction, and imposing the leader's own opinions and ideas as to how the activity should develop.

Creative drama groups have potential with many sorts of client including chronic groups in long stay wards, more able mentally handicapped people and those people with specific physical dys-functions.

Focus on Tasks, Skills and Learning

In a group of this nature, the behaviour and skills of everyday life can be rehearsed and refined or modified through the medium of drama in a variety of activities such as role play. Some skills develop as a by-product of creative drama work; other programmes must be specifically designed. Skills acquired may include simple communication or training in the use of non-verbal signs; initiating conversation; or improving conceptual skills like problem solving. Group members can gain experience of decision making and negotiation; and begin to develop some autonomy as well as co-operative skills. This drama work is very goal specific; and it is often developed, for example, in rehabilitation groups in prisons, psychiatric hospitals, children's homes.

The work planned for a group with a focus on 'skills' is likely to form one part of an overall programme of training or education; and in such a group, the leader's role as 'model' is especially important.

Focus on Insight, Self Awareness and Change

Here, the focus is again entirely different. An 'insight-type' group would be set up for the benefit of particular clients such as acute admissions groups and those people in family and marital therapy (or indeed all those groups already mentioned).

Within the context of the group, unconscious processes may be given creative expression by enacting scenes from past, present and future, and sometimes by recreating the themes of dreams and fantasies. The drama activities selected for work of this kind give members an opportunity to explore their own feelings and relationships within the security of the group.

All the work on role play and media skills which may be used by the 'creative' drama group may also be used here. However, it is understood in an 'insight' group that self discovery and change are the aims and that, for this purpose, the group represents 'life', the family or the outside world. Members are encouraged to reflect on

6

their own experiences, and the group also becomes the scenario within which possible changes can be explored. By use of symbolism, certain mental or physical blocks may be resolved through new insights and increased confidence.

The leader will be likely to run such a group as a 'closed' group, namely to make it available only to the original membership who should remain constant in the relatively long-term. Depending upon the degree of experience of the leader and the rationale of the group, 'interpretation of experiences' may or may not be emphasised. Often, gradually emerging conscious awareness of previously unacknowledged difficulties, *without* the use of verbal analysis or interpretation, proves to be of greatest value.

Before Setting Up a Group

Rationale and objectives

Before embarking on the detailed planning which is involved in setting up any group activity, it is as well to give careful thought to the rationale of a potential drama group, and to administrative considerations. The following questions are intended to alert the reader to possible pitfalls and to help in ascertaining the leader's main objectives.

Why	
Why start a group in the first place?	Has a need been established? Are the staff skills available? Are there suitable clients?
Why choose drama rather than other skills or creative processes?	Are there specific or general goals? Is the work experimental? Research? Is drama the main focus for therapy? or is it a support therapy?

What	
What model of group will it be?	Will it be open to new members? Will it be a closed group from the outset?
What emphasis will the group have?	Will it focus on creativity, tasks or insight? (See p. 5-6)
What numbers are planned?	Will there be a fixed number? Should a minimum or maximum number be set? *(10 is a good size for a group: severely handicapped people need smaller groups)*
What staff ratio is planned?	Will there be a single leader? Will there be a co-leader? Will there be assistants/students?
What will be the role of assistants/students in relation to the clients?	Should they interact in the group in the same way as clients? Will they act purely as assistants to the leader?
What will be the duration of the group?	Will it span 10 weeks; 20 weeks; a year? *(If possible, avoid open-ended arrangements)*
What will be the frequency and length of sessions?	1 hour twice a week? 1 ½ hours once a week? *(See Planning and Preparation)*
What sort of records will be kept of individuals or group activities?	Will these be formal or informal? Will video or written notes be used? Remember to record and monitor *your* feelings and processes.

How	
How will members be recruited to the group?	By self-referral?
How will people know about the group?	By publicity or a talk? Via the referring agent? Via a noticeboard or announcement?
How will people be selected for the group?	Open to all comers? By interview? By medical or other selection?
How will aims and goals be established?	Will they be fixed by the leader? Will they be negotiable? (See Page 20)
How will this group relate to the overall workload?	Will it be unconnected? Will it be an integral part of a programme? Will it overcrowd other work?
How will breaks for illness or holidays be covered?	Natural breaks? Substitute leader available? Co-leader available?

Where	
Where will the group be held?	Are you responsible for a space? Must space be negotiated? Is there a suitable space?
Where are the emergency facilities?	Where is the First Aid Box? Where is the spare key? Where is the Fire Extinguisher/Fire Escape?
Where will the leader find support?	Are colleagues available? Can friends provide support?

Who	
Who will provide supervision?	Will this come from outside? Will the institution provide it? Will it be individual or in a group setting?
Who is responsible for the management and organisation of the group?	The institution? The team? The leader?
Who co-ordinates the overall treatment programme?	The institution? The team? The leader?

Clarifying Aims

Whilst considering what type and focus of group is required, and having worked through administrative and other details, it is also advisable for the leader to be clear about the overall aims for the group. It has been found from experience that conflicts can arise if the aims of the institution and the group members are not compatible with those of the leader.

The following simple chart has been devised to assist in identifying potential areas of dissonance *before* the group is set up. The reader may wish to redesign the chart or the headings.

Clarifying Aims	
A. My aims for the group	B. The institution's aims for the group
C. The group's aims for themselves	D. My aims for myself

A sample follows of how this chart has been used in practice:

A.	B.
1. Provide a structure for change	1. Keep group meaningfully busy
2. Develop trust and co-operation	2. Avoid confrontation; keep atmosphere calm
3. Develop communication	3. Maintain status quo
C.	D.
1. Relieve boredom	1. Develop work professionally
2. Feel better	2. Feel satisfaction at achieving aims
3. Sleep properly	3. Develop myself

The reader is invited to consider the above chart where we see that the aims of A and C are not wholly incompatible. The aims of A and B, however, might give rise to conflict (viz. A1 in direct opposition to B3). The leader can reflect on how, for example, D3 can be achieved; and whether the potential difficulties identified could be avoided.

It should be pointed out that, with certain groups, it may be more appropriate to clarify further details of aims in discussion with group members during the first session.

Supervision and Training

Supervision and Support

As previously mentioned, to achieve the best results in creative drama, regular supervision is essential. Because of the nature of this work, a leader may tend towards over-involvement, excessive use of energy, and a counter-productive degree of identification with members of the group. Supervision, by providing support and feedback, helps keep all the processes moving forwards and enables the leader to discuss details, to plan ahead and to function with the right degree of compassionate detachment.

Supervision should be provided by an experienced person, preferably a senior working colleague; and it may have to be sought if it does not exist.

Support networks may be both professional and social and are also very important. The leader of a group should be sure to make regular opportunities for 'switching off' from work. A more balanced outlook on the activities of a group and on work in general can be achieved if there are creative or other activities to occupy one's leisure time.

Training

If any professional is interested in pursuing creative drama work with groups, some specific training is warmly recommended. Training courses, whilst limited in their locations, are increasing in number. Those who have already taken a dramatherapy course are encouraged to attend for further training in order to extend their range of skills. Courses of varying lengths are run at the following addresses:

▶ **Dramatherapy Consultants,** 6 Nelson Avenue, St Albans, Herts AL1 5RY (publications, short courses, on-going groups and supervision).

▶ **Herts College of Art and Design,** 7 Hatfield Road, St Albans, Herts (post-graduate training, summer schools and short courses).

▶ **College of Ripon and York St John,** Lord Mayor's Walk, York (post-graduate training, summer schools and short courses).

▶ **London Drama and Tape Centre,** 11 Princeton Street, London WC1 (drama workshops; library and tape service and publications).

▶ **British Association for Dramatherapists,** PO Box 98, Kirbymoorside, York YO6 6EX (conferences and publications).

▶ **South Devon Technical College,** Torquay (part-time courses).

Some Words of Caution

When running a creative drama group we must bear in mind that all therapies can occasionally stimulate unexpected reactions to particular techniques. Dramatherapy is no exception; indeed it may give rise to some unhelpful results in certain circumstances.

Whilst it is not realistic to hope to cover every contingency in a book of this size, some essential basic guidelines are given below. The reader is reminded that it is always advisable to obtain regular supervision and that advice should be sought if a leader is in any doubt about an activity or the behaviour of an individual group member.

General advice

▶ Guard against thinking of drama simply as a collection of techniques. Remember it is a *creative process* which can tap experience at a very profound level.

▶ *Never* introduce a new idea or activity to a group without having tried it out. Always experiment first on yourself and colleagues.

▶ Develop 'antennae' and be sensitive to the group's changing needs and moods. Members will often know 'where they need to go' and what they are ready for, even if they cannot yet verbalise it.

▶ Aim to act as a catalyst rather than a controller. Be alert to this situation and avoid using phrases such as "we've *got* to do this"; "I'll *make* them do that" or "They *have* to . . ."

Situations to handle with special care

▶ Highly stimulating material is not appropriate for severely disturbed, maladjusted or hyperactive groups.

▶ When initiating role play remember that to 'be someone else' can be a very disturbing experience for clients who are not comfortable in their own identity.

▶ Appearing to 'get lost in an activity' is not necessarily an indication of fruitful involvement.

▶ An apparently cathartic group experience is not always an indication of a 'good' session. And the evidence of catharsis is not necessarily a highly visible expression of emotion.

▶ Direct techniques such as spectograms (see pages 24-25) can be unhelpful to some people because the end product may be perceived as reinforcing the unsatisfactory present rather than pointing to a hopeful future.

13

N.B. Semi-hypnotic techniques such as deep relaxation or guided fantasy are not dealt with here since they are only appropriately applied in controlled settings by highly trained professionals.

Planning and Preparation

It is a mistake to imagine that what may appear to be an informal, unstructured, creative drama session needs no pre-planned framework. The most successful sessions are those which have a beginning, a middle and an end; which are kept to a pre-arranged time; and in which the leader maintains an imperceptible yet confident 'steadying hand' on the way group activities evolve.

When planning for creative drama work, a leader should first endeavour to find a suitable setting for the group. This need not be luxurious. In fact carpets, for example, are a handicap. However, it is helpful to have sufficient space, light and some fresh air. A wooden or cork tile floor is ideal; and easy chairs or rostra are preferable to either upright chairs or floor cushions because they are both more relaxing and more flexible. Good lighting is also an asset.

Preparation for drama sessions requires considerable fore-thought. It is necessary to decide upon an overall framework for work with the group so that it develops sequentially and ideas are linked from session to session.

The great advantage of structure is that, within it, there can be flexibility. Each group is like a living, growing organism which responds to its members and its leader who are also living, changing organisms. A leader develops the capacity to respond to the needs and mood of the group through his or her own spontaneity and creativity. Initially, the inexperienced will rely heavily on detailed planning of each session. However, in time and with practice, this structure can be allowed greater flexibility as the leader puts increasing trust in intuition and judgement.

The diagram opposite illustrates how a session can be planned. The ideal session length for a group of 10 clients is 1½ hours. Within this span adequate time must be allowed for warming-up or *'opening'* activities, for *'development'* which involves the main work of the session, and for a satisfactory and relaxed winding-up or *'closure'*.

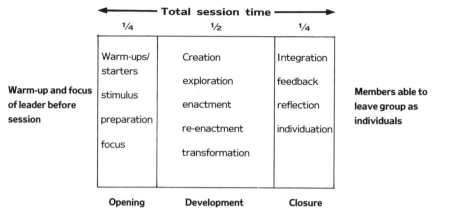

| | Total session time | | |
	¼	½	¼
Warm-up and focus of leader before session	Warm-ups/ starters stimulus preparation focus	Creation exploration enactment re-enactment transformation	Integration feedback reflection individuation	**Members able to leave group as individuals**
	Opening	**Development**	**Closure**

Even before the session begins, the leader must make time to warm-up and 'focus', in other words to get emotionally and mentally prepared for action.

Vitality and a sense of purpose must be conveyed to the group when they first arrive. They should be greeted with an air of warmth and confidence, for some may be feeling nervous, anxious or even antagonistic. Time should not be wasted before embarking on the appropriate warm-up or starter activities such as are described in Part II. This opening phase, which should last not more than one quarter of the total session, involves stimulation and preparation for the development phase, and begins to focus attention on the area of work to be covered.

The development phase should span not more than half of the total session time. Within the space of perhaps ¾ hour, the group may be active in creating a story, mask or scene; in exploring feelings, a theme or a topic (perhaps through improvisation); in either exploratory or goal-specific role play (*enactment*); or in re-enacting an experience which may be either invented or real, myth or fantasy.

The leader will have selected games or other activities through which some, but by no means all, of the above can be developed.

15

For some groups, or in some sessions, this will be a time for exploring and working on change in members' feelings (*transformation*).

For the final quarter of the session, more restful exercises are chosen through which the group can make a gradual transition from the focus of the session back to the focus of everyday activities. Material and feelings which have been put in focus must now be 're-owned' (*integration*). New insights are absorbed and group members are encouraged to reflect on what has taken place rather than only to rely on feedback from others (*reflection*). These two processes may not necessarily occur within a group session but time and space must nonetheless be provided for that possibility.

Techniques of distancing and relaxing may be employed in order to help members reconstrue themselves as separate individuals who relate to, but are not fused with, the group (*individuation*).

Finally, when the session is brought to a close (*on time*, and gently but firmly), each member should be in a frame of mind which enables him/her to leave as an individual in a relaxed manner. After the session, a leader should make some notes on what took place, what exercises were used, and what reactions they produced. Leaders should also learn to monitor their own reactions, bodily feelings, and record the 'process' of the group.

Sample Sessions

The following sample sessions suggest how a group session may be 'thought through', with different exercises being selected according to needs. They also show how the same techniques may be used to respond to different needs.

It should be stressed that the three examples offer no more than guidelines and should not therefore be interpreted as set formulae.

▶ **Example 1**
Creative expressive focus
Elderly institutionalised group
Duration of session: 1 hour
Grouping: 6-8 people

Aims and objectives	To counteract institutionalisation; to provide a physical stimulus; to emphasise identity; to reinforce simple choices; and to encourage creativity.
Warm up phase	Physical: 'Stretch and Shake' (cf. Warm ups No. 16, p 50). Music may be helpful here (eg. Walk in the Black Forest). Names: 'Name Volley' or 'Name Likes' (cf. Names Nos. 1 and 2, pages 35 and 36). These exercises need reinforcing and may slowly be made more difficult.
Development phase	Exercises selected will depend how familiar the group is with drama activities. The above exercises may be sufficient during early sessions; closing with a quiet relaxation activity such as 'Recapitulation' No. 8, p 182. Start simply with the basic exercise then develop improvisation, eg. "Who is ringing up? Have they some special news?" Alternatively, in groups of three, think of a situation when the telephone rings at just the wrong moment.
Closure phase	Relaxation (No. 5, p. 179)

▶ **Example 2**
Task centred focus
Rehabilitation prisoners group
Duration of session: 1½ hours
Grouping: 10 people

Aims and objectives	To develop flexibility in dealing with various situations; to prepare for return to life 'outside'; to experience managing rather than being managed; and to develop trust and communication skills.
Warm up phase	Physical: 'Energy Focus' (cf. Warm ups No. 12, p. 46). Trust: 'Group Fall' (cf. Warm ups No. 9, p. 43)

Develop- **ment** **phase**	Goal-specific role play: 'Saying No' or 'Persuasion' (cf. Improvisation and Role Play Nos. 24 and 25 (p. 130-131).
Closure **phase**	'Feedback' (cf. Closures No. 12, p. 186). Allow members of the group to discuss how they felt during the exercises and to consider whether comparisons can be drawn with feelings they have experienced before.

▶ **Example 3**
Insight type
Disturbed children
Duration of session: 1 hour
Grouping: 4 people

Aims and **objectives**	To develop awareness whilst taking into account hostility towards families which may not have been verbalised. To limit work to the one-hour session, since anxiety levels may be high; and to increase members' trust in their peers and their leader.
Warm up **phase**	Names: 'Name Stories' (cf. Warm ups No. 4, p. 38) Trust: 'Group Fall' (cf. Warm ups No. 9, p. 43)
Develop- **ment** **phase**	Visual dynamics: 'Spectograms' (cf. Visual dynamics, No. 12, p. 154) If a high level of anxiety is apparent, then animals may be used first in play. Later, the story of the animals may be told, *rather than* specifically working with 'my family'.
Closure **phase**	De-roling. Here, a variation on 'de-roling from roles' may be used. Allow the 'animals' to become ordinary animals again before they are put away: this may be achieved through play or discussion. Movement (cf. Closures No. 3, p. 177).

Equipment

Things to acquire

Creative drama requires little in the way of elaborate props or expensive equipment. However, a sturdy tape or record deck (which has the right adaptor and one knows how to work!) is a valuable asset. A selection of tapes and/or records should be carefully chosen for appropriate movement and relaxation exercises. In addition, it is helpful to have a supply of large sheets of paper, a quantity of felt tip pens, an unlimited supply of newspapers and some large cardboard boxes. For role play exercises it may be appropriate to accumulate a general 'dressing up' collection including a wide variety of hats and caps and perhaps some chiffon strips and scarves.

A range of toys, zoo and farm animals and a box of miscellaneous small objects can be used in creating spectograms and pictograms; and stiff card and some craft materials would be needed if the group were working with masks.

For further equipment suggestions, Chapter II of 'Remedial Drama' (Jennings, 1978) is recommended.

Things to make

Puppets and masks should, wherever possible, be made with the group and not *for* them. This may, however, be impractical, for severely handicapped people, for example.

Simple role play cards, to accompany some of the exercises described in Part II, can be made very easily by using small library cards which are convenient to store. Print in large and clear letters with a dark felt pen, putting one phrase on each card. For example, write a stimulating opening line on each card: "We had just settled down for tea when there was a knock at the door . . ."

Simpler cards can be prepared for those who are not ready for full role play exercises. In this case, elements of a role can be identified and a variety of feelings, for example, can be written on separate cards. When each member has taken a card, individuals may be asked to imagine, "How do I *sit* with this feeling?" or "How do I *look* with this feeling?" (An example of this type of activity can be found in Part II, No. 3, p. 109.)

Pair cards are versatile additions to basic resources. Using these, characters may be asked to 'find' each other in a game or role play (eg. mother/father/baby; farmer/cow; master/slave). A propos of the latter type of activity, male/female options should be kept open and stereotypes avoided wherever possible. Pair cards can also be used when comparing and contrasting feelings such as happy/sad; or when looking at qualities and characteristics in improvisations (eg. "I like to be in charge"/"I like to be told what to do").

Negotiating a Contract

At the first official session, although individuals may have been previously interviewed and the general purpose of the group discussed, the leader should spend perhaps half of the time developing a rapport with the group, giving necessary information and agreeing a contract with the members. This contract should encompass what is expected of the group but should also take into account what the leader has to offer to them.

A positive working alliance must be established between the group and its leader in this first session; and this can be achieved by discussing and agreeing on its direction and specific aims. In the absence of such an alliance, co-operation from individual members cannot be guaranteed. Experience has shown that negative feelings may later be transferred to the leader, or certain group members may resort to 'acting out'. Naturally, the level of discussion and the flexibilty of the contract must depend upon the type of setting and the nature of the clients. If the verbal skills of the group are limited, it may be helpful to use 'action method' to work out the contract (eg. role play illustrating punctuality or confidentiality). If this is the case, then a smooth transition must be achieved between this introductory activity and the rest of the session.

Many operational details need to be agreed; and the leader is advised to prepare a mental list of matters to raise informally with the group. A list of possible issues for consideration is provided below. This is intended purely as a guideline.

Points to raise and discuss with the group

1. What are the aims and intentions of the group? *(Goals)*
2. How will the group achieve those aims? *(Methods)*
3. What has the leader in terms of skills and experience that could be beneficial to the group and vice versa? *(Expectations)*
4. What does it mean to have an 'open'/'closed' group? *(Framework)*
5. If it is a closed group, how are leaving and entry to be agreed? *(Negotiation)*
6. Does 'anything go' or are there limits on behaviour eg. aggression? *(Boundaries)*
7. What should be the starting and finishing times? *(Punctuality)*
8. What is agreed about smoking/refreshments, etc? *(Ground rules)*
9. What happens to personal information/photographs etc? *(Confidentiality)*
10. How will ground rules and limits be maintained? *(Consensus)*

Opening a Session

Having given careful thought to various aspects of the group, as outlined in earlier sections, and having planned an appropriate mix of activities for the current session, one final piece of preparation is advised. In order to gain members' interest and co-operation from the moment they arrive, the leader needs to make mental preparation beforehand. For, just as a 'cold' group tends to be unresponsive until it is 'warmed up', so the leader must warm up too. This is achieved by allowing sufficient time to think about the group, to re-read notes from the previous session, to consider what was achieved and to identify other themes which may be appropriate to explore. All other preoccupations should be put to one side while a group is in progress.

On the arrival of participants, a short time generally needs to be spent on 'starter' or 'warm up' activities. These may serve as a preparation for the main business of the session, in which case the tone and type of exercises chosen will need to be compatible with the main focus. Warm ups may also be used as an initial focus for members, particularly if the group arrives already warmed up but with animation and energy which would benefit from being channelled into some kind of structure.

Depending upon the nature and mood of the group, these introductory exercises may be used for warming up voices, reactions or general creativity; or they may serve as 'getting to know you' activities. When used in this way they might be described as providing a stimulus for the group.

Once the session is under way, the leader should 'listen' to the group's verbal and non-verbal messages, assessing their mood and noticing their reactions to activities, to the leader and to each other. Themes, too, may emerge naturally and can be incorporated into the work of the session by a perceptive leader.

If the current mood of the group is, for example, wary, then warm ups may be used either to work with that mood or to dispel it, or to explore it. Likewise, fearful, 'tight' or anticipatory moods can be worked into the framework of the session if the leader remains responsive to the needs of the group. On occasion, a high level of anxiety may be noted at the beginning of a session, and some work on breathing and relaxation may be chosen to occupy the warm-up phase.

As a general rule, starters should be consistent with the overall strategy. Therefore, if a quiet reflective atmosphere is required because the development phase is to be spent creating spectograms (see p. 24-25), noisy or very physical warm ups would naturally be inappropriate. If whole group, small group or paired work is planned, then warm ups can lay the foundations for this.

A word of advice in relation to the latter: do not make the mistake of asking a group to form pairs when there are are an uneven number of participants! If pairs are essential then solve the dilemma by offering to be someone's partner.

Opening exercises are described in Part II, under the following headings. The reader is advised to select one or two according to the various criteria discussed above, and bearing in mind the type of group, number of members, overall programme of work and current needs.

I	Names
II	Trust
III	Physical
IV	Breathing and Vocal
V	Feelings
VI	Action/Interaction

Developing a Session

Once a group has been warmed up and is beginning to focus on a theme, a task or an issue, the leader may use a range of methods to develop the session. This middle phase should not occupy more than half of the total session time.

In choosing activities, the leader not only takes into account whether the group is focusing on creativity, tasks or insight (cf. p 5-6) but should also consider 'where the group is at'. For example, a warm up may have produced an unexpected result — an exercise may have been too difficult, leaving the group feeling somewhat inadequate (de-skilled). In this situation, it would be necessary to shift focus slightly and to build up group confidence again by re-working that warm up in a different way.

The group may have arrived with 'left over business' from another situation or from the previous week's session. That, too, might require attention perhaps in the development phase. If, however, the group appears ready to proceed, then activities may be structured in one of the following ways.

Creativity and Expression

When stimulating creativity, themes such as 'the sea' (cf. p. 111) may be explored through movement; they may be dramatised through an improvisation; or they may be created in a drama or a

23

text (eg. Sea Fever by John Masefield). Finally, they may be refined through a performance.

Tasks and Skills
Working towards specific goals such as the achievement of listening or 'looking' skills, tasks may be practised in very small steps, eg. gradually encouraging eye contact in one who finds it extremely difficult. Example: the I-Spy game (p. 90) involves both listening and looking. Alternatively, they may be structured within a game (cf. 1-2-3-Change places, p. 81) or rehearsed through simulation, by re-creation of the real life situation.

Insight and Awareness
Issues such as positive self image or family relationships may be explored through sculpting (cf. p. 25), worked with through role play or transformed into an improvisation, a story or a myth.

To summarise then, a wealth of techniques may be employed to facilitate development of a session. It is essential to *contain* what is developed, not using too many techniques and allowing time for assimilation of the experience and for integration.

An explanation of some activities may be helpful at this point. A large selection of games is included here because of their great versatility. Games provide a sense of security and structure; and they help to build up confidence and skills in a group. On occasion, they may simply be used for their own sake — for example in new groups or when light relief is considered appropriate. After improvisation, role play or work with masks, adequate time should be allowed for de-roling. Role reversals are often helpful for adding new insights.

Sculpts and spectograms are valuable visual presentations of situations, which may make an individual's path seem clearer.

24

However, they should be used judiciously for they have an immediacy as techniques, making them inappropriate where a member, for example, construes his life as 'empty'. Sufficient time must always be made available for support and follow-up after such exercises. Sculpts may be used for decision making, problem solving, or simply for reflecting the status quo. They are found helpful to individuals, to families and to whole groups. Spectograms, too, provide a simple visual medium whereby life pictures can be created using a range of small objects. Participants are encouraged not to be too literal in what they select to represent people, key objects, ambitions, emotions, etc.

Development exercises are described in Part II, grouped under the following headings:

GAMES
I   Co-operative
II   Competitive
III Concentration
IV   Guessing/memory
V   Conceptual
VI   Community

IMPROVISATION AND ROLE PLAY
I   Role play preparation
II   Improvisation
III Simulation — life and social skills
IV   Family role play

VISUAL DYNAMICS
I   Sculpting
II   Spectograms
III Pictograms
IV   Family trees
V   Masks

Closing a Session

A leader must learn to sense the appropriate moment at which to start 'closing' a session. It is ill-advised to over-run the planned time and then to say, three minutes before the end "It's time for us to stop". However, beware of interrupting a valuable piece of work that is proving very absorbing or intense, simply to impose an ending on the session. It is the leader's responsibility to bring about a 'de-climax', gradually working towards the closure. If members are deeply involved in an activity they should be brought slowly 'to the surface'. For example, if people are engaged in improvisation, they should be warned in good time . . . "You have five minutes more, then we shall present this work to the other group members".

During effective closure exercises, each individual de-intensifies the experiences of the session. This may in some instances be achieved through gentle relaxation. Members should be encouraged to integrate their experiences through reflection. Reflection may often encompass their 'life as a whole' and not simply the experience of that session.

Any involvement in role play *must* include a 'de-roling' process (cf. p. 175) whereby individuals acknowledge that they are 'themselves' again. Group members usually wish to share their experiences and may also give feedback to others. This should not, however, feel like an obligation. Each participant should be able to leave the group feeling he or she has a separate identity from other group members. This is what is described on page 16 as individuation, and involves facilitation of distancing and leaving.

Closure exercises are described in Part II under the following headings:

I	De-roling
II	Relaxation
III	Guided Focus
IV	Feedback
V	Movement
VI	Diaries
VII	Ritual

References

(Space does not allow a comprehensive reading list. Relevant and full bibliographies are supplied in the books marked*)

Barker, C. *Theatre Games*, Methuen, 1978.

Blatner, H. *Acting In*, Springer, 1973.

Burr, L. (ed). *Therapy Through Movement*, Winslow Press, 1986.

Brudenell, P. *The Other Side of Profound Handicap*, Macmillan, 1986.

Cox, M. *Structuring the Therapeutic Process*, Pergamon, 1978.

Cox, M. *Coding the Therapeutic Process*, Pergamon, 1978.

Goffman, E. *Presentation of self in everyday life*, Penguin, 1967.

***Jennings, S.** *Remedial Drama*, A. & C. Black, 1973.

***Jennings, S. (ed).** *Creative Therapy*, Kemble Press, 1975.

Jennings, S. Beware of drama, in *Journal of Dramatherapy*, Vol. 3, No. 2, 1979.

Jennings, S. Models of Practice in dramatherapy, in *Journal of Dramatherapy*, Vol. 7, No. 1, 1983.

Jennings, S. (ed). *Dramatherapy: Theory and Practice*, Croom Helm, 1987.

O'Neill, C. and Lambert, A. *Drama structures*, Hutchinson, 1982.

Scher, A. *The Year of the King*, Chatto, 1985.

Dramatherapy Journal, published by BADTH, PO Box 98, Kirby-moorside, Yorkshire.

Drama Therapy Bulletin, published by Dramatherapy Consultants, 6 Nelson Avenue, St Albans AL1 SRY.

Part II
Creative Drama Methods

Introduction

Visual Dynamics / 143

CLOSURE PHASE

Closures / 175

Appendix

Notes

Introduction

The second half of this book is devoted to creative drama exercises. Whilst some are specific to an area of work or type of group, others have a more general usage. For specific guidance on how to select appropriate activities, please refer to Planning and Preparation, page 14.

Layout

The OPENINGS section (coloured pink) covers all types of starters and warm ups. The DEVELOPMENT section (coloured salmon) includes Games, Improvisation and Role Play (coloured yellow) and Visual Dynamics (coloured green). Finally the CLOSURES section (coloured blue) provides a range of exercises with which the leader may bring a session to a relaxed and satisfying conclusion. Some blank pages are provided at the end of the book for readers' notes.

Key

The reader will note that a key is supplied on each page. It should be stressed that the classification is not rigid, for most activities are versatile and could be modified. An example of a Key and its interpretation are provided below to illustrate how it may be used in session planning.

Key	
Focus	*Creativity* ☑ *Skills* ☐ *Insight* ☑
Grouping	*Whole Group* ☐ *2* ☐ *3* ☐ *4* ☑ *5* ☑
Time	*5-10 min* ☐ *10-15 min* ☐ *15-20 min* ☑
Anxiety	*Low* ☑ *Medium* ☐ *High* ☐
Music	*Helpful* ☑ *Not relevant* ☐
R.P.P.	*Useful for Role Play Practice* ☑

Thus the above activity is likely to be most appropriate to groups focusing on Creativity and Expression or Insight and Self Awareness. It is an exercise suited to 'family' groups of four or five and will take some time to develop. It should not therefore be combined with another lengthy activity in the 'Development' phase. Only a low level of anxiety is likely to be engendered; the use of suitable music may enhance the exercise; and the tasks involved make it an ideal preparation for future role play work.

Openings

WARM UPS AND STARTERS

I: Names

1: Name Volley

This activity involves the use of a soft ball or bean bag and may be played with the group either seated or standing.

Each person calls his or her own name as he/she throws the ball to another member of the group.

Pause after several turns, and see how many names people can remember.

Development/variations:
(i)   Invite people to throw the ball and call the name of the person they are throwing it to.
(ii) Ask people to make a comment about themselves as they throw the ball.
(iii) Invite them to throw the ball and make an observation about the person they are throwing it to.
(iv) Invite them to call out a name yet throw the ball to the person *on that person's right* (very challenging!).

Key	
Focus	*Creativity* ☑ *Skills* ☑ *Insight* ☑
Grouping	*Whole Group* ☑ *2* ☐ *3* ☐ *4* ☐ *5* ☐
Time	*5-10 min* ☐ *10-15 min* ☑ *15-20 min* ☐
Anxiety	*Low* ☑ *Medium* ☐ *High* ☐
Music	*Helpful* ☐ *Not relevant* ☑
R.P.P.	*Useful for Role Play Practice* ☑

WARM UPS AND STARTERS

I: Names

2: Name Likes

Ask group members to sit in a circle and take turns to think of a food which has the same initial letter as their first name.
Examples:

My name is Sue and I like strawberries.

My name is Matthew and I like meringues.

My name is John and I like jacket potatoes.

Development/variations:

(i)   In place of foods, use TV programmes or colours etc:
e.g. My name is Mary and I like Duran Duran.

(ii)   Each person can introduce the person *before* them, and then make their own contribution:
e.g. Your name is Pat and you like Coronation Street. My name is Robert and I like Match of the Day.

(iii) When all members have been given the opportunity to introduce themselves, see if one person can remember *everyone's* contributions.

Key	
Focus	*Creativity* ☑ *Skills* ☑ *Insight* ☑
Grouping	*Whole Group* ☑ *2* ☐ *3* ☐ *4* ☐ *5* ☐
Time	*5-10 min* ☐ *10-15 min* ☐ *15-20 min* ☑
Anxiety	*Low* ☑ *Medium* ☐ *High* ☐
Music	*Helpful* ☐ *Not relevant* ☑
R.P.P.	*Useful for Role Play Practice* ☐

WARM UPS AND STARTERS

I: Names

3: Name Movement

Ask members to stand in a circle. This activity will require careful explanation. Instruct members to take turns to step into the centre of the circle and give their names as they make a clear gesture or movement of their choice.

The whole group echoes both the name and the movement, then the individual repeats both in response to the group, and then the group echo a *second* time.

Development/variations:
(i)   Use the same format but invite each member to make up a name he or she would like.
(ii) Use all the above movements as the basis for a choreographed 'dance'.
(iii) Use the names of the group to devise a rhythmic chant to which all members can move, perhaps clicking their fingers to keep in rhythm.

Key	
Focus	*Creativity* ☑ *Skills* ☐ *Insight* ☐
Grouping	*Whole Group* ☑ *2* ☐ *3* ☐ *4* ☐ *5* ☐
Time	*5-10 min* ☑ *10-15 min* ☐ *15-20 min* ☐
Anxiety	*Low* ☐ *Medium* ☐ *High* ☑
Music	*Helpful* ☑ *Not relevant* ☐
R.P.P.	*Useful for Role Play Practice* ☐

WARM UPS AND STARTERS

I: Names

4: Name Stories

Ask the group to divide into pairs or small groups and sit in a circle. Instruct members to tell their partner or group *why* they have their name. Can they think of other people who share their name? Are any of them famous? Would they have chosen that name for themselves? What alternative might they choose?

Development/variations:

(i) Ask individuals to imagine a famous person with their name and tell the story of that person.

(ii) Discuss surnames. Who would like to change their surname? Who knows what their surname means?

(iii) Consider why some people choose to change their surnames. Who can think of any examples? What are members' opinions?

Key	
Focus	*Creativity* ☑ *Skills* ☑ *Insight* ☐
Grouping	*Whole Group* ☐ *2* ☑ *3* ☑ *4* ☐ *5* ☐
Time	*5-10 min* ☐ *10-15 min* ☑ *15-20 min* ☐
Anxiety	*Low* ☐ *Medium* ☑ *High* ☐
Music	*Helpful* ☐ *Not relevant* ☑
R.P.P.	*Useful for Role Play Practice* ☐

WARM UPS AND STARTERS

I: Names

5: Name Guess

With the group sitting or standing in a circle, members are asked to look around the group and guess anyone's name. Each one should say why he or she thought of that particular name.

Development/variations:

(i)   Invite each person in turn to tell the group his or her initials. See if the group can guess the names.

(ii) Invite each person to think of a 'special' middle name he or she would choose. See if the others can guess what it is.

(iii) Invite either the group or the individual to think of an adjective (with the same initial letter) which would go with each member's first name.
e.g. Laughing Laura, Sad Sarah, Happy Henry.

Key	
Focus	*Creativity* ☑ *Skills* ☑ *Insight* ☑
Grouping	*Whole Group* ☑ *2* ☐ *3* ☐ *4* ☐ *5* ☐
Time	*5-10 min* ☐ *10-15 min* ☑ *15-20 min* ☐
Anxiety	*Low* ☐ *Medium* ☑ *High* ☐
Music	*Helpful* ☐ *Not relevant* ☑
R.P.P.	*Useful for Role Play Practice* ☐

WARM UPS AND STARTERS

I: Names

6: Name Meaning

In this final activity associated with names, members are invited to tell the group the meaning of their name, if they know it. (The group leader may find it helpful to obtain a book on names and their meanings.)

Each person should have an opportunity to say if their name feels right for them "today" or "every day". Does a name need a certain mood?

Development/variations:

(i)   Discuss which country or county each member's name comes from. Do the family still live near their roots?

(ii) Elaborate on the theme of names by exploring comparable first names in other languages, and deciding which people prefer, e.g. Frances and Françoise.

Key	
Focus	*Creativity* ☐ *Skills* ☑ *Insight* ☐
Grouping	*Whole Group* ☑ *2* ☐ *3* ☐ *4* ☐ *5* ☐
Time	*5-10 min* ☑ *10-15 min* ☐ *15-20 min* ☐
Anxiety	*Low* ☑ *Medium* ☐ *High* ☐
Music	*Helpful* ☐ *Not relevant* ☑
R.P.P.	*Useful for Role Play Practice* ☐

WARM UPS AND STARTERS

II: Trust

7: Trust Walk

Ask the group to divide into pairs, numbering themselves '1' and '2'. The '1's close their eyes, and the '2's are instructed to take the '1's for a gentle walk. Explain that eyes should remain closed until they are asked to open them, that the pairs should not talk to each other while the Trust Walk is in progress, and that it is best for the 'guide' to hold his or her partner's arm or shoulder.

Development/variations:
(i)   Invite the 'guides' to describe to their partners the scenes where they are being led.
(ii) Ask half the group to close their eyes *before* being allocated a partner. At the end of the Trust Walk, can each guess who their partner was?

Key	
Focus	*Creativity* ☑ *Skills* ☑ *Insight* ☐
Grouping	*Whole Group* ☐ *2* ☑ *3* ☐ *4* ☐ *5* ☐
Time	*5-10 min* ☐ *10-15 min* ☐ *15-20 min* ☑
Anxiety	*Low* ☐ *Medium* ☑ *High* ☐
Music	*Helpful* ☐ *Not relevant* ☑
R.P.P.	*Useful for Role Play Practice* ☐

WARM UPS AND STARTERS

II: Trust

8: Trust Fall

Important:
This exercise must not be hurried nor be allowed to get silly. If it is not taken seriously, it loses its value. The group divides into pairs, spaced well apart, one person standing firmly behind the other. *Keeping body and legs straight* the person in front falls backwards against the supporting hands of the partner behind.

As trust builds up, the partner behind stands, progressively, a little further away. It may be helpful to demonstrate this with a colleague. The partner behind 'catches' the other's shoulders and stands them upright again. Give each partner a turn at 'falling'.

Key	
Focus	*Creativity* ☑ *Skills* ☑ *Insight* ☐
Grouping	*Whole Group* ☐ *2* ☑ *3* ☐ *4* ☐ *5* ☐
Time	*5-10 min* ☐ *10-15 min* ☐ *15-20 min* ☑
Anxiety	*Low* ☐ *Medium* ☑ *High* ☐
Music	*Helpful* ☐ *Not relevant* ☑
R.P.P.	*Useful for Role Play Practice* ☐

WARM UPS AND STARTERS

II: Trust

9: Group Fall

Important:
This exercise *must* be taken seriously and should progress through small, gradual steps, as in exercise 8.

Instruct the group to stand shoulder to shoulder forming a tight circle, with one person standing in the centre.

The individual in the centre closes his or her eyes and, standing with legs and body quite straight, 'falls' towards the circle. Members of the circle support and push the person upright again.

Give each individual a turn in the centre; to minimize anxiety of not being 'caught' and supported adequately, confidence should be built up gradually.

Key	
Focus	*Creativity* ☐ *Skills* ☐ *Insight* ☑
Grouping	*Whole Group* ☑ *2* ☐ *3* ☐ *4* ☐ *5* ☑
Time	*5-10 min* ☐ *10-15 min* ☐ *15-20 min* ☑
Anxiety	*Low* ☐ *Medium* ☐ *High* ☑
Music	*Helpful* ☐ *Not relevant* ☑
R.P.P.	*Useful for Role Play Practice* ☐

WARM UPS AND STARTERS

II: Trust

10: Group Lift

Ask one member of the group to lie on the floor with eyes closed. Instruct the remaining group members how to lift that person up to waist level by careful co-ordination; and to rock him or her gently before lowering the person to the ground. The group should remain with the individual at ground level until he or she has opened his/her eyes.

Important: be sure that the head is always higher than the feet, to avoid giddiness. And make it very clear that the following variations should be planned with care and total concentration.

Development/variations:

(i) For a celebratory lift, raise the individual above the heads of the group.

(ii) To explore risk-taking, gently 'toss' the individual.

(iii) Explore how many different ways the group can lift one person.

Key	
Focus	*Creativity* ☑ *Skills* ☐ *Insight* ☑
Grouping	*Whole Group* ☑ *2* ☐ *3* ☐ *4* ☐ *5* ☑
Time	*5-10 min* ☐ *10-15 min* ☐ *15-20 min* ☑
Anxiety	*Low* ☐ *Medium* ☐ *High* ☑
Music	*Helpful* ☐ *Not relevant* ☑
R.P.P.	*Useful for Role Play Practice* ☐

WARM UPS AND STARTERS

II: Trust

11: Back Lift

The ideal number for this exercise is 6. Ask 5 members to go down on hands and knees, to position themselves very close together, and to form a 'back' across which the sixth person can lie with his or her eyes closed.

When all are in position, the 'back' rocks gently to and fro in a co-ordinated manner. The individual may choose whether to lie prone or supine.

Development/variations:

(i)   Suggest that members of the 'back' move their own spines up and down gently, thus providing a human massage.

(ii) Encourage the group to find a creative way for the person to get off the 'back', eg. everyone lie flat so he/she can roll off.

(iii) Invite the 'back' to move smoothly together across the room, giving the individual a ride.

NB: Let each member have a turn on the 'back'.

Key	
Focus	*Creativity* ☑ *Skills* ☐ *Insight* ☑
Grouping	*Whole Group* ☑ *2* ☐ *3* ☐ *4* ☐ *5* ☐
Time	*5-10 min* ☐ *10-15 min* ☐ *15-20 min* ☑
Anxiety	*Low* ☐ *Medium* ☑ *High* ☐
Music	*Helpful* ☑ *Not relevant* ☐
R.P.P.	*Useful for Role Play Practice* ☐

WARM UPS AND STARTERS

III: Physical

12: Energy Focus

Instruct the group that they have *one* minute in which to:
   "Touch four corners of the room; the floor; and six pairs of knees".
   Indicate when 50 seconds have elapsed, and when the time is up.
   Then invite the group to retrace their steps exactly. Can they remember whose knees they touched, and in what order?

Development/variations:
(i)   A variation for less mobile individuals is to ask the group to "touch your head; your knees; and hold the hands of the person next to you". No time limit is imposed here.
(ii) Ask the group to "touch the floor; the ceiling; all corners of the room; and then 'hide' under a chair". This variation is popular with high energy groups!

Key	
Focus	*Creativity* ☑ *Skills* ☑ *Insight* ☐
Grouping	*Whole Group* ☑ *2* ☐ *3* ☐ *4* ☐ *5* ☐
Time	*5-10 min* ☑ *10-15 min* ☐ *15-20 min* ☐
Anxiety	*Low* ☑ *Medium* ☐ *High* ☐
Music	*Helpful* ☐ *Not relevant* ☑
R.P.P.	*Useful for Role Play Practice* ☐

III: Physical

13: Head to Toe

Give the group the following explanation: "I am going to call out two body parts. Let one part of *you* touch the *other* part of someone else, eg. if I call out 'thumbs to waist', *your* thumbs must touch the waist of someone else".

This activity can be developed according to the abilities and mobility of the group, ie. "head to toe" for flexible, energetic people; "bottom to toe" for relaxed and mobile people!

Let group members call out their own suggestions.

Development/variations:
(i)   hand to head; elbow to shoulder; chin to knee etc.
(ii) body parts matching — knee to knee, finger to finger etc.
(iii) *all* hands touching; *all* feet touching etc.

Key	
Focus	*Creativity* ☑ *Skills* ☐ *Insight* ☐
Grouping	*Whole Group* ☑ *2* ☐ *3* ☐ *4* ☐ *5* ☐
Time	*5-10 min* ☑ *10-15 min* ☐ *15-20 min* ☐
Anxiety	*Low* ☑ *Medium* ☐ *High* ☐
Music	*Helpful* ☐ *Not relevant* ☑
R.P.P.	*Useful for Role Play Practice* ☐

III: Physical

14: Colour Touch

Introduce this exercise in the following way:

"I am going to call out two colours. Touch *one* of those colours on yourself and one on someone else" eg. "brown and blue": I can touch *my* brown hair and *his* blue shirt".

When the group have become accustomed to this, invite individuals to call out colour pairs. (The leader may like to rehearse this activity by first calling out only one colour.)

Development/variations:
(i)   Ask members to touch *both* colours on others, and not on themselves.
(ii) Try introducing three colours.
(iii) Vary the activity by touching colours anywhere in the room.

Key	
Focus	*Creativity* ☑ *Skills* ☑ *Insight* ☐
Grouping	*Whole Group* ☑ *2* ☐ *3* ☐ *4* ☐ *5* ☐
Time	*5-10 min* ☑ *10-15 min* ☐ *15-20 min* ☐
Anxiety	*Low* ☑ *Medium* ☐ *High* ☐
Music	*Helpful* ☐ *Not relevant* ☑
R.P.P.	*Useful for Role Play Practice* ☐

WARM UPS AND STARTERS

III: Physical

15: Colour Choice

It is often helpful to introduce this exercise through general discussion on colours. Look around the room at the group members' clothing: how many colours are there?

Ask the group to scatter around the room, perhaps in pairs, and call out instructions to them, eg. "Touch a colour that you like, on someone else: tell that person why you like it".

Development/variations:
(i) Call out one/two/three colours and ask the group to find them somewhere around the room.
(ii) Invite pairs to share with each other their favourite colours, and what they would choose in those colours, eg. clothes; furniture; food.
(iii) Encourage pairs to discuss what they wore as children; school uniform; best clothes. Did they like them?

Key	
Focus	*Creativity* ☑ *Skills* ☑ *Insight* ☐
Grouping	*Whole Group* ☑ *2* ☑ *3* ☐ *4* ☐ *5* ☐
Time	*5-10 min* ☐ *10-15 min* ☐ *15-20 min* ☑
Anxiety	*Low* ☑ *Medium* ☐ *High* ☐
Music	*Helpful* ☐ *Not relevant* ☑
R.P.P.	*Useful for Role Play Practice* ☐

WARM UPS AND STARTERS

III: Physical

16: Stretch and Shake

This exercise tones up the whole system very effectively.

Ask members of the group to stretch up and stretch right through their bodies, but *without* raising their shoulders. Then tell them to give a big yawn.

Repeat this, ensuring that all joints remain loose.

After stretching, ask members to begin to shake each part of their bodies, beginning with the hands. Keep all these movements *loose*, checking for tension, eg. at the back of the neck.

Even the head can be shaken, but warn the group not to strain or be too vigorous. Be watchful that knee joints are not tensed.

Key	
Focus	*Creativity* ☑ *Skills* ☐ *Insight* ☐
Grouping	*Whole Group* ☑ *2* ☐ *3* ☐ *4* ☐ *5* ☐
Time	*5-10 min* ☐ *10-15 min* ☐ *15-20 min* ☑
Anxiety	*Low* ☑ *Medium* ☐ *High* ☐
Music	*Helpful* ☑ *Not relevant* ☐
R.P.P.	*Useful for Role Play Practice* ☐

WARM UPS AND STARTERS

III: Physical

17: Statue Shapes

Precede this exercise by warming up gently with rhythmic movement to music, or perhaps by using exercise 16, then invite the group to walk briskly around the room, weaving in and out of each other to form patterns on the floor.

This activity often needs some practice in order to encourage people to use their bodies.

Warn the group that the leader will stop them periodically and call out a *shape*, which they must try to make with their bodies eg. round, spiky, straight etc.

Development/variations:
(i)   See if they can make that shape in pairs.
(ii) See if they can make the shape in '3's.

Key	
Focus	*Creativity* ☑ *Skills* ☑ *Insight* ☐
Grouping	*Whole Group* ☑ *2* ☑ *3* ☑ *4* ☐ *5* ☐
Time	*5-10 min* ☑ *10-15 min* ☐ *15-20 min* ☐
Anxiety	*Low* ☑ *Medium* ☐ *High* ☐
Music	*Helpful* ☐ *Not relevant* ☑
R.P.P.	*Useful for Role Play Practice* ☐

WARM UPS AND STARTERS

III: Physical

18: Statue Movements

This exercise should begin as for exercise 17, with members walking briskly around the room.

Instruct the group as follows: "When I say stop — stand still and listen to me. I shall call out a movement which I want you to do until I instruct you to start walking again."

Development/variations:
(i) Invite members to make the movements with a partner.
(ii) Let others call out movements spontaneously.
(iii) Structure the activity so each member can call out a movement, taking turns.
(iv) Encourage the group to put the movements together to form a sequence, perhaps to music.

Key	
Focus	*Creativity* ☑ *Skills* ☐ *Insight* ☐
Grouping	*Whole Group* ☑ *2* ☐ *3* ☐ *4* ☐ *5* ☐
Time	*5-10 min* ☐ *10-15 min* ☐ *15-20 min* ☑
Anxiety	*Low* ☑ *Medium* ☐ *High* ☐
Music	*Helpful* ☑ *Not relevant* ☐
R.P.P.	*Useful for Role Play Practice* ☐

WARM UPS AND STARTERS

III: Physical

19: Pushing and Pulling

This activity uses 'energy' and also helps to focus attention on people's bodies and balance.

At first, the group may be rather afraid of their own strength and hold back from taking it seriously.

Invite members to choose a partner, face each other, and put their hands on each others' shoulders. Ask them to see if they can push each other across the room. Discourage frivolity, by helping members to explore real energy and the importance of balance.

Development/variations:
(i)   Partners can hold each other's hands and attempt to *pull* rather than push across the room, using their feet to grip on the floor.
(ii) Let them try arm wrestling, either on the floor or on a chair.
(iii) Let them hold only *one* hand, and take turns to pull and be pulled. This encourages timing and general body control.

Key	
Focus	*Creativity* ☑ *Skills* ☑ *Insight* ☐
Grouping	*Whole Group* ☐ *2* ☑ *3* ☐ *4* ☐ *5* ☐
Time	*5-10 min* ☐ *10-15 min* ☐ *15-20 min* ☑
Anxiety	*Low* ☑ *Medium* ☐ *High* ☐
Music	*Helpful* ☐ *Not relevant* ☑
R.P.P.	*Useful for Role Play Practice* ☐

WARM UPS AND STARTERS

III: Physical

20: Walking

This activity encourages expansion of movement and the varying of rhythm.

Ask the group to walk round the room at their normal walking pace, in and out, avoiding touching anyone. They are to *freeze* when given the signal to do so. A drum is helpful in this exercise.

Then ask the group to try walking at *twice* the speed, still without touching or bumping into anyone. Again to *freeze* when given the signal to do so.

Development/variations:
(i)   Suggest that the group walk in *slow motion* and glide in and out. Freeze.
(ii)   Finally, can they *creep* round the room, so that movement is almost imperceptible.

These can all be repeated in different sequences.

Key	
Focus	*Creativity* ☑ *Skills* ☑ *Insight* ☐
Grouping	*Whole Group* ☑ *2* ☐ *3* ☐ *4* ☐ *5* ☐
Time	*5-10 min* ☑ *10-15 min* ☐ *15-20 min* ☐
Anxiety	*Low* ☑ *Medium* ☐ *High* ☐
Music	*Helpful* ☐ *Not relevant* ☑
R.P.P.	*Useful for Role Play Practice* ☐

III: Physical

21: Circles and Lines

Instruct the group to walk briskly around the room; then to
freeze. Instruct them to continue walking, but this time in
straight lines only (making sharp turns) and — *freeze*. Finally,
ask them to walk only in curved lines, walking smoothly round
people. And — *freeze*.

Development/variations:
(i)   Suggest that members try standing on the spot and move
      parts of their bodies either in straight lines or in circles etc.
(ii) Suggest dividing into pairs or small groups, standing on the
      spot, and some making straight lines while others make
      curves.
(iii) Experiment with making a 'mobile' together, using patterns
      of lines and curves.

Key	
Focus	*Creativity* ☑ *Skills* ☑ *Insight* ☐
Grouping	*Whole Group* ☑ *2* ☑ *3* ☑ *4* ☑ *5* ☑
Time	*5-10 min* ☐ *10-15 min* ☑ *15-20 min* ☐
Anxiety	*Low* ☐ *Medium* ☑ *High* ☐
Music	*Helpful* ☐ *Not relevant* ☑
R.P.P.	*Useful for Role Play Practice* ☐

WARM UPS AND STARTERS

III: Physical

22: Gravity Jump

A warm up is necessary before attempting this exercise; warm up nos. 16, 19 and 20 are recommended.

Divide the group into threes, with the two outer partners each holding an arm of the person in the centre. The middle person is assisted in jumping higher and higher, starting from *very* low; remember that this may be an unnerving experience for some people.

Important:
This exercise is not as simple as it seems. It takes time for a group of three to learn to coordinate their rhythm; it is helpful to suggest a count of "1, 2, 3, up".

Each member of the group should be given the opportunity to jump.

Key	
Focus	*Creativity* ☑ *Skills* ☐ *Insight* ☐
Grouping	*Whole Group* ☐ *2* ☐ *3* ☑ *4* ☐ *5* ☐
Time	*5-10 min* ☐ *10-15 min* ☑ *15-20 min* ☐
Anxiety	*Low* ☐ *Medium* ☑ *High* ☐
Music	*Helpful* ☐ *Not relevant* ☑
R.P.P.	*Useful for Role Play Practice* ☐

III: Physical

23: Group Flying

This activity is not unlike some trust exercises, for it requires the group to have confidence in each other; and it involves some risk taking.

The object is for a group (maximum 6) to carry one person around the room as if they were flying — face downwards and with arms outstretched like wings. Explain that great care *must* be taken, and that the pace should begin very slowly and gradually increase. The latter creates a sense of exhilaration.

Each member of the group should be given an opportunity to 'fly'; but no-one should be forced to do so.

Key	
Focus	*Creativity* ☑ *Skills* ☐ *Insight* ☐
Grouping	*Whole Group* ☑ *2* ☐ *3* ☐ *4* ☐ *5* ☐
Time	*5-10 min* ☑ *10-15 min* ☐ *15-20 min* ☐
Anxiety	*Low* ☐ *Medium* ☐ *High* ☑
Music	*Helpful* ☐ *Not relevant* ☑
R.P.P.	*Useful for Role Play Practice* ☐

WARM UPS AND STARTERS

IV: Breathing and Vocal

24: Yawning and Sighing

The group can sit or stand for this exercise. Ask them to do a huge, *silent* yawn; then to yawn and allow a modest sound to come out; and finally to yawn *very noisily*.

Next, show the group how to breathe in through the nose and give a sigh; then breathe in and sigh longer; and finally to exaggerate this by making a loud noise.

Development/variations:

(i)   Divide into pairs and ask one person to yawn while the other sighs at her partner.

(ii) Divide the group in half and instruct one half to yawn then make a pre-arranged sound (eg. groaning, fearful, dragon-like etc.) The other half of the group guess what sort of noise it is meant to be.

Key	
Focus	*Creativity* ☑ *Skills* ☑ *Insight* ☐
Grouping	*Whole Group* ☑ *2* ☑ *3* ☐ *4* ☐ *5* ☑
Time	*5-10 min* ☑ *10-15 min* ☐ *15-20 min* ☐
Anxiety	*Low* ☑ *Medium* ☐ *High* ☐
Music	*Helpful* ☐ *Not relevant* ☑
R.P.P.	*Useful for Role Play Practice* ☐

WARM UPS AND STARTERS

IV: Breathing and Vocal

25: Deep Breaths

It is best to ask the group to stand for this activity. However, for some it may be easier to sit.

Demonstrate how to breathe in through the nose to a count of 3 — hold the breath for 3 — and breathe out to a count of 3. Explain that, when breathing naturally, we pause between inhalation and exhalation.

Important:
Warn members against tensing their necks or raising their shoulders when breathing in deeply.

Development/variations:
(i) Gradually expand the count, eg. Breathe in -2-3-4-5; hold it -2-3-4-5; and now breathe out -3-4-5.
(ii) To provide a contrast with the above, suggest breathing in *sharply*; holding; and then breathing out sharply through the mouth, using 'Ha!'.

Key	
Focus	*Creativity* ☑ *Skills* ☑ *Insight* ☐
Grouping	*Whole Group* ☑ *2* ☐ *3* ☐ *4* ☐ *5* ☐
Time	*5-10 min* ☑ *10-15 min* ☐ *15-20 min* ☐
Anxiety	*Low* ☑ *Medium* ☐ *High* ☐
Music	*Helpful* ☐ *Not relevant* ☑
R.P.P.	*Useful for Role Play Practice* ☐

WARM UPS AND STARTERS

IV: Breathing and Vocal

26: Humming

Ask members to breathe in then start to hum very quietly, getting gradually louder, and finish before they begin to feel uncomfortable.

Reverse this process: breathe in deeply, start humming very loudly and gradually diminuendo as the breath runs out.

Development/variations:
(i)   Suggest that members hum with a partner, forehead to forehead and then cheek to cheek, to try to *feel* the vibrations they create. The greater the oral resonance, the more vibration they will feel.
(ii) Ask the group to hum up and down the scale, discovering how high and how low each one can reach.

Key	
Focus	*Creativity* ☑ *Skills* ☑ *Insight* ☐
Grouping	*Whole Group* ☑ *2* ☑ *3* ☐ *4* ☐ *5* ☐
Time	*5-10 min* ☑ *10-15 min* ☐ *15-20 min* ☐
Anxiety	*Low* ☐ *Medium* ☑ *High* ☐
Music	*Helpful* ☐ *Not relevant* ☑
R.P.P.	*Useful for Role Play Practice* ☐

WARM UPS AND STARTERS

IV: Breathing and Vocal

27: The Balloon

First, as a whole group, mime blowing up a balloon until it is large. Tie the top. Count to 3. Then burst it!

Next, invite people to imagine themselves as balloons. Crouch low on the floor, and grow bigger and rounder with each imaginary puff.

Divide members into pairs, and get one partner to be a balloon whilst the other inflates them. Synchronise the bursting of all the balloons eg. "Tie the top; find a pin; 1, 2, 3 — BANG!" 'Balloons' then slowly deflate and relax. Give both partners a chance to be the balloon.

Development/variations:
(i) Put one half of the group in the centre of the circle, and blow them all up and burst them.
(ii) Blow some people up into interesting shaped balloons which must be led carefully home so they don't burst.

Key	
Focus	*Creativity* ☑ *Skills* ☑ *Insight* ☐
Grouping	*Whole Group* ☑ *2* ☑ *3* ☐ *4* ☑ *5* ☑
Time	*5-10 min* ☑ *10-15 min* ☐ *15-20 min* ☐
Anxiety	*Low* ☐ *Medium* ☑ *High* ☐
Music	*Helpful* ☐ *Not relevant* ☑
R.P.P.	*Useful for Role Play Practice* ☐

WARM UPS AND STARTERS

IV: Breathing and Vocal

28: Resonators

Leaders will find that many people need some help to 'expand' their vocal capacity and the ability to resonate.

First, ask the group members to breathe in deeply, *without* raising their shoulders. They should then simply try humming until the breath runs out.

Next, ask them to take a good deep breath, hum as before, and beat the chest with the flat of the hand, to 'encourage' the sound. This can be repeated using alternative 'mm' and 'ah' sounds.

Development/variations:

(i)   Divide into pairs so that one partner can strike the other on the back with the flat of the hand to 'encourage' either 'mm' or 'ah' sounds.

(ii)   Experiment with Tarzan cries whilst beating the chest with alternate fists, Tarzan-style.

Key	
Focus	*Creativity* ☑ *Skills* ☑ *Insight* ☐
Grouping	*Whole Group* ☑ *2* ☑ *3* ☐ *4* ☐ *5* ☐
Time	*5-10 min* ☑ *10-15 min* ☐ *15-20 min* ☐
Anxiety	*Low* ☐ *Medium* ☑ *High* ☐
Music	*Helpful* ☐ *Not relevant* ☑
R.P.P.	*Useful for Role Play Practice* ☐

WARM UPS AND STARTERS

IV: Breathing and Vocal

29: Tongue Twisters

To encourage concentration and articulatory coordination, invite the group to try some of the following. Work up from the very simple to more difficult examples:

"Thursday, Friday, Saturday, Sunday" (in chorus, all together)

"The tip of the tongue and the teeth and the lips" (together, and then individually)

"Red leather, yellow leather" (together)

"A laurel crowned clown" (individually)

"Sister Suzie stitches socks for saucy sailors" (individually)

Ask members to contribute their own favourites.

Key	
Focus	*Creativity* ☐ *Skills* ☑ *Insight* ☐
Grouping	*Whole Group* ☑ *2* ☐ *3* ☐ *4* ☐ *5* ☐
Time	*5-10 min* ☑ *10-15 min* ☐ *15-20 min* ☐
Anxiety	*Low* ☐ *Medium* ☑ *High* ☐
Music	*Helpful* ☐ *Not relevant* ☑
R.P.P.	*Useful for Role Play Practice* ☐

V: Feelings

30: Seasons and Celebrations

Give the group a framework within which to begin to describe their own feelings. Sit in a circle, and introduce discussion of the seasons and of different celebrations.

Ask each member to think of a time of year they particularly like or dislike and to complete the following sentence:

"I like . . . because it reminds me of when I . . . (eg. went to the seaside))" or

"I don't like . . . because it reminds me of when . . . (eg. my brother was taken ill)".

Development/variations:
(i)   Use the above to lead into more detailed discussion of seasons, of celebrations, or of more general likes and dislikes.
(ii) Can group members remember a birthday they particularly enjoyed and one they did not?

Key	
Focus	*Creativity* ☐ *Skills* ☐ *Insight* ☑
Grouping	*Whole Group* ☑ *2* ☐ *3* ☐ *4* ☐ *5* ☐
Time	*5-10 min* ☑ *10-15 min* ☑ *15-20 min* ☐
Anxiety	*Low* ☑ *Medium* ☑ *High* ☐
Music	*Helpful* ☐ *Not relevant* ☑
R.P.P.	*Useful for Role Play Practice* ☐

WARM UPS AND STARTERS

V: Feelings

31: Feeling good/Feeling bad

This exercise is similar to no. 30 in that it involves making comparisons. Ask the group to sit in a circle and encourage them to share some positive and negative feelings, first by using a set structure:

"I feel good when I . . ."

"I feel bad when I . . ."

eg. "I feel good when I am out walking."

"I feel bad when I can't relax."

Development/variations:

(i) Once the set pattern has ceased to be a necessary stepping-stone, encourage further discussion of these feelings where appropriate.

(ii) Vary the 'feeling' words to include eg. fearful/confident; embarrassed/comfortable.

Key	
Focus	*Creativity* ☐ *Skills* ☐ *Insight* ☑
Grouping	*Whole Group* ☑ *2* ☐ *3* ☐ *4* ☐ *5* ☐
Time	*5-10 min* ☑ *10-15 min* ☑ *15-20 min* ☐
Anxiety	*Low* ☐ *Medium* ☑ *High* ☐
Music	*Helpful* ☐ *Not relevant* ☑
R.P.P.	*Useful for Role Play Practice* ☐

WARM UPS AND STARTERS

IV: Feelings

32: Feeling Words

For this activity, participants will require felt pens and cards.

Ask members to write down as many 'feeling' words — one per card — as they can think of, and to put the cards in a pile. Then ask the whole group to cooperate in sorting these into smaller piles under different headings, eg. 'temperature' (hot/cold/warm feelings); 'illness' (unwell, poorly); 'moods' (bored, elated, cheerful).

This exercise leads to some debate on what feelings belong in what categories.

Development/variations:
(i)   Examine how many different, yet *similar*, words there are.
(ii) Identify those which occur most often. Do these reflect the current mood of the group, perhaps?
(iii) Each pick a card at random and try to describe that feeling.

Key	
Focus	*Creativity* □ *Skills* ☑ *Insight* ☑
Grouping	*Whole Group* ☑ *2* □ *3* □ *4* □ *5* □
Time	*5-10 min* □ *10-15 min* ☑ *15-20 min* □
Anxiety	*Low* □ *Medium* ☑ *High* □
Music	*Helpful* □ *Not relevant* ☑
R.P.P.	*Useful for Role Play Practice* □

WARM UPS AND STARTERS

V: Feelings

33: What affects Feelings?

This activity provides an opportunity for further verbal interaction. It may take the form of constructing verbal pictures, or it may develop into a full discussion. Explore with the group what varied factors may change people's feelings eg. weather, colours, time of day/week/month, events etc.

Perhaps make a chart to include everyone's contributions and explore what people have in common.

Development/variations:

(i)   Introduce a discussion on the lines of: "What clothes do I feel happy/not happy in?"

(ii) Introduce a discussion on the lines of: "What place or places do I feel happy/not happy in?"

Key	
Focus	*Creativity* ☐ *Skills* ☑ *Insight* ☑
Grouping	*Whole Group* ☑ *2* ☑ *3* ☐ *4* ☐ *5* ☐
Time	*5-10 min* ☐ *10-15 min* ☑ *15-20 min* ☐
Anxiety	*Low* ☐ *Medium* ☑ *High* ☑
Music	*Helpful* ☐ *Not relevant* ☑
R.P.P.	*Useful for Role Play Practice* ☐

WARM UPS AND STARTERS

V: Feelings

34: Who affects Feelings?

Develop discussion of feelings by considering how other people affect the way we feel.

Ask members to contribute one negative and one positive statement to illustrate the above eg. I always *feel irritated* when I see my mother; I always *feel pleased* when I see my son.

Important:
It may be helpful to many groups to begin with less specific examples eg. "People younger than me make me *feel* nervous; people older than me make me *feel* safe."

Development/variations:
Cut out pictures to make a collage of people members do and don't like.

Key	
Focus	*Creativity* ☐ *Skills* ☑ *Insight* ☑
Grouping	*Whole Group* ☑ *2* ☑ *3* ☐ *4* ☐ *5* ☐
Time	*5-10 min* ☐ *10-15 min* ☑ *15-20 min* ☐
Anxiety	*Low* ☐ *Medium* ☑ *High* ☑
Music	*Helpful* ☐ *Not relevant* ☑
R.P.P.	*Useful for Role Play Practice* ☐

WARM UPS AND STARTERS

V: Feelings

35: Foods and Feelings

Ask members of the group in turn to say *one positive* and *one negative* thing about any food or drink eg. I *love* jelly but I *hate* spinach!

Suggest that each speaker really exaggerates the words *love* and *hate*. The subject of food invariably gives rise to animated discussion which may be structured more or less by the leader if considered appropriate.

Development/variations:

Ask each member in turn to try inverting his or her first statement, pretending to *love* all the food they dislike, and vice versa!

Key	
Focus	*Creativity* ☐ *Skills* ☐ *Insight* ☑
Grouping	*Whole Group* ☑ *2* ☐ *3* ☐ *4* ☐ *5* ☐
Time	*5-10 min* ☑ *10-15 min* ☐ *15-20 min* ☐
Anxiety	*Low* ☐ *Medium* ☐ *High* ☑
Music	*Helpful* ☐ *Not relevant* ☑
R.P.P.	*Useful for Role Play Practice* ☐

WARM UPS AND STARTERS

VI: Action/Interaction

36: On the Spot

Before the session, the leader will need to prepare a series of cards on which are printed some awkward questions eg.:

"I am your landlady — where is the rent?"

"I am a father — have you been seeing my daughter?"

"I am a policeman — may I ask you a few questions about last night?"

Ask the group to sit in a circle. Give each person a card and invite them to ask 'their' question of the person next to them. *No-one is required to answer the question — simply to listen.*

Development/variations:
(i)   Each person *may* answer the question, but in one or two words only; in one sentence only.
(ii) Encourage the group to ask all of the questions as if they were very old; very young; a foreigner.

Key	
Focus	*Creativity* ☐ *Skills* ☑ *Insight* ☐
Grouping	*Whole Group* ☑ *2* ☐ *3* ☐ *4* ☐ *5* ☐
Time	*5-10 min* ☐ *10-15 min* ☑ *15-20 min* ☐
Anxiety	*Low* ☑ *Medium* ☐ *High* ☐
Music	*Helpful* ☐ *Not relevant* ☑
R.P.P.	*Useful for Role Play Practice* ☑

VI: Action/Interaction

37: Opposites

Before the session, it is necessary to prepare a series of role cards which could be arranged into pairs eg:

> policeman: criminal
> lost child: worried parent
> nurse: man with crutches

When each member has been given a card he or she should first 'become' that person and then try to find the individual with whom he/she may be paired.

Development/variations:

(i) Suggest that members pair randomly and strike up an appropriate conversation eg. policeman and man with crutches; lost child with criminal; nurse with worried parent.

Key	
Focus	*Creativity* ☐ *Skills* ☑ *Insight* ☐
Grouping	*Whole Group* ☐ *2* ☑ *3* ☐ *4* ☐ *5* ☐
Time	*5-10 min* ☐ *10-15 min* ☑ *15-20 min* ☐
Anxiety	*Low* ☐ *Medium* ☑ *High* ☐
Music	*Helpful* ☐ *Not relevant* ☑
R.P.P.	*Useful for Role Play Practice* ☑

WARM UPS AND STARTERS

VI: Action/Interaction

38: Salesperson

This activity may be introduced either through role cards or by verbal instruction. The topic under consideration is that of *persuasion*.

Divide the group into pairs so that one partner can *attempt* to persuade the other to buy something conventional, such as a vacuum cleaner. The 'customer', in turn, may be instructed to be either disinterested or over-enthusiastic.

Development/variations:
(i) Follow the same procedure, but selling something silly yet making it sound serious.
(ii) Experiment with trying to collect money for a new charity, yet getting the same negative responses.
(iii) Invite members to try selling a new brand of washing powder, using as many 'scientific' words as possible.

Key	
Focus	*Creativity* ☐ *Skills* ☐ *Insight* ☑
Grouping	*Whole Group* ☐ *2* ☑ *3* ☐ *4* ☐ *5* ☐
Time	*5-10 min* ☑ *10-15 min* ☐ *15-20 min* ☐
Anxiety	*Low* ☐ *Medium* ☑ *High* ☐
Music	*Helpful* ☐ *Not relevant* ☑
R.P.P.	*Useful for Role Play Practice* ☑

WARM UPS AND STARTERS

VI: Action/Interaction

39: Two minute Interviews

Before the session, the leader may wish to prepare some cards describing different people eg. an old lady who has just won the pools; a fireman who has just saved a child in an accident. Divide the group into pairs, and invite partners to take turns to interview each other:
either on something that is familiar eg. their favourite TV programme
or on something unexpected or extraordinary eg. "I hear you have just invented . . . .. Will you tell the viewers about it?"

Important:
With practice, 'interviewers' will learn to ask helpful questions should 'interviewees' get stuck.

Development/variations:
Will you tell me the story of your life — in 2 minutes?"

Key	
Focus	*Creativity* ☐ *Skills* ☑ *Insight* ☐
Grouping	*Whole Group* ☐ *2* ☑ *3* ☐ *4* ☐ *5* ☐
Time	*5-10 min* ☑ *10-15 min* ☐ *15-20 min* ☐
Anxiety	*Low* ☐ *Medium* ☑ *High* ☐
Music	*Helpful* ☐ *Not relevant* ☑
R.P.P.	*Useful for Role Play Practice* ☑

WARM UPS AND STARTERS

VI: Action/Interaction

40: Telephone Talk

This exercise works best with the group sitting in a circle. A model telephone may be helpful. Instruct members that they will be required to 'ring up' the person sitting next to them, using a set format eg. "My name is . . . and I'm saying hello to . . . "

The next person around the circle repeats what has gone before, and then gives his own 'message' eg. "David said hello to Paul. Paul said hello to me. My name is Mary and I'm saying hello to June."

This becomes increasingly difficult to remember!

Development/variations:

(i)   After saying hello, each member adds a personal message.
(ii) After saying hello, give some news or ask to borrow something.

Key	
Focus	*Creativity* ☐ *Skills* ☑ *Insight* ☐
Grouping	*Whole Group* ☑ *2* ☐ *3* ☐ *4* ☐ *5* ☐
Time	*5-10 min* ☐ *10-15 min* ☑ *15-20 min* ☑
Anxiety	*Low* ☐ *Medium* ☑ *High* ☐
Music	*Helpful* ☐ *Not relevant* ☑
R.P.P.	*Useful for Role Play Practice* ☑

Development Phase

GAMES

I: Co-operative

1: Balloons

If possible, each member of the group is given a large, strong balloon to blow up; this provides good breathing practice for those who would benefit from it.

See if each individual can keep a balloon in the air, either by blowing or by patting with the hand, from a sitting position or when standing.

Development/variations:
(i) Divide members into pairs and invite them to keep balloons airborne by their joint efforts.
(ii) Provide a very large, strong balloon for the whole group to endeavour to keep in the air.

Key	
Focus	*Creativity* ☑ *Skills* ☐ *Insight* ☐
Grouping	*Whole Group* ☑ *2* ☐ *3* ☐ *4* ☐ *5* ☐
Time	*5-10 min* ☐ *10-15 min* ☐ *15-20 min* ☑ *15-20 min* ☐
Anxiety	*Low* ☑ *Medium* ☐ *High* ☐
Music	*Helpful* ☐ *Not relevant* ☑
R.P.P.	*Useful for Role Play Practice* ☐

GAMES

I: Co-operative

2: Pass balloon/Pass ball

For this exercise, only one balloon or ball is required (though one or two spare balloons are advisable!).

Using only one hand, group members pass the balloon from one to the other trying not to drop it.

Development/variations:
(i)   Each person passes the balloon or ball *from one hand to the other* before passing it on.
(ii) Try holding the balloon between the *knees* and passing it on that way.
(iii) Hold a ball or balloon under the *chin* and pass it on that way.

Key	
Focus	*Creativity* ☑ *Skills* ☑ *Insight* ☐
Grouping	*Whole Group* ☑ *2* ☐ *3* ☐ *4* ☐ *5* ☐
Time	*5-10 min* ☑ *10-15 min* ☐ *15-20 min* ☐
Anxiety	*Low* ☑ *Medium* ☐ *High* ☐
Music	*Helpful* ☐ *Not relevant* ☑
R.P.P.	*Useful for Role Play Practice* ☐

GAMES

I: Co-operative

3: Newspaper Game

Place the same number of sheets of newspaper on the floor as there are small groups. Invite members to fit all of their group on to their sheet without tearing the paper.

Development/variations:
(i)   Make the pieces of newspaper progressively smaller.
(ii) Use the 'islands' of paper for a variation on musical chairs.
(iii) Exchange the newspaper for a hoop to stand in.

Key	
Focus	*Creativity* ☑ *Skills* ☐ *Insight* ☐
Grouping	*Whole Group* ☐ *2* ☐ *3* ☑ *4* ☑ *5* ☑
Time	*5-10 min* ☐ *10-15 min* ☑ *15-20 min* ☐
Anxiety	*Low* ☐ *Medium* ☑ *High* ☐
Music	*Helpful* ☐ *Not relevant* ☑
R.P.P.	*Useful for Role Play Practice* ☐

GAMES

I: Co-operative

4: Body Parts

For this exercise groups of five or six are ideal. Instructions must be given carefully and adequate time must be allowed.

Explain that parts of the body have a specific number value — "Backs count as 1; hands count as 5; feet are 1 each; and bottoms count as 2."

See if the group can continue to have body parts representing a *maximum* of 6 points, touching the floor eg. two feet, two backs and one bottom; necessitating that two group members be raised above the floor in some ingenious way.

Development/variations:
(i)   Reduce the maximum number of points allowed, and see how ingenious and trusting members become.
(ii) Vary the body parts; or the numbers in the groups.

Key	
Focus	*Creativity* ☑ *Skills* ☑ *Insight* ☐
Grouping	*Whole Group* ☑ *2* ☐ *3* ☐ *4* ☐ *5* ☑
Time	*5-10 min* ☐ *10-15 min* ☑ *15-20 min* ☐
Anxiety	*Low* ☐ *Medium* ☑ *High* ☐
Music	*Helpful* ☐ *Not relevant* ☑
R.P.P.	*Useful for Role Play Practice* ☐

GAMES

I: Co-operative

5: One, Two, Three

This is an entertaining game which requires concentration.

Members should stand in a circle for this activity. Everyone counts "1, 2, 3" in unison and then each looks at someone else in the circle. Should any two people find they are looking at each other, then they change places.

Development/variations:
(i) Give each member a hat to wear. If two people find they are looking at each other, then they change places *and* hats.
(ii) After each "1, 2, 3" any group members who are changing places can call out 'Hippopotamus' whilst those who are not moving call out 'Rhinoceros'.

Key	
Focus	*Creativity* ☑ *Skills* ☑ *Insight* ☐
Grouping	*Whole Group* ☑ *2* ☐ *3* ☐ *4* ☐ *5* ☐
Time	*5-10 min* ☑ *10-15 min* ☐ *15-20 min* ☐
Anxiety	*Low* ☑ *Medium* ☐ *High* ☐
Music	*Helpful* ☐ *Not relevant* ☑
R.P.P.	*Useful for Role Play Practice* ☐

GAMES

I: Co-operative

6: *Pass the Orange*

This is an old Victorian party game. Do not introduce the activity to a very new group, for members may get anxious about touching each other.

Demonstrate how to hold an orange firmly under the chin and pass it on to someone else *without* using your hands.

Arrange the group in a circle, and see if the orange can travel right round the group without being either handled or dropped.

Development/variations:

Divide members into two teams and see which can move the orange fastest, without dropping it.

NB: Let this game stay fun, and avoid it becoming too competitive.

Key	
Focus	*Creativity* ☑ *Skills* ☐ *Insight* ☐
Grouping	*Whole Group* ☑ *2* ☐ *3* ☐ *4* ☐ *5* ☐
Time	*5-10 min* ☑ *10-15 min* ☐ *15-20 min* ☐
Anxiety	*Low* ☐ *Medium* ☑ *High* ☐
Music	*Helpful* ☐ *Not relevant* ☑
R.P.P.	*Useful for Role Play Practice* ☐

GAMES

I: Co-operative

7: Pairs

Before the session prepare cards of paired items such as:

| fish | + | chips | | upstairs | + | downstairs |

It should first be ascertained that all group members can read.
Physical and vocal warm ups are generally necessary before this
exercise.

Shuffle and deal the cards, and invite members to find their
pairs by shouting out the word on their card.

Development/variations:

(i)   The same game can be played, using opposites instead of
      paired words eg.

| hot | + | cold | | tidy | + | untidy |

(ii) Play the paired words game, this time asking members not
      to *talk*, but to *move* as their word. (This inevitably gives rise
      to some hilarity!)

(iii) Invite the group to make up and use their own cards.

Key	
Focus	*Creativity* ☑ *Skills* ☑ *Insight* ☐
Grouping	*Whole Group* ☑ *2* ☑ *3* ☐ *4* ☐ *5* ☐
Time	*5-10 min* ☑ *10-15 min* ☐ *15-20 min* ☐
Anxiety	*Low* ☐ *Medium* ☑ *High* ☐
Music	*Helpful* ☐ *Not relevant* ☑
R.P.P.	*Useful for Role Play Practice* ☑

GAMES

I: Co-operative

8: Trinomials

Warm up the group with a vocal exercise such as 26 or 29 then ask members to arrange themselves in groups of 3. Suggest they try to think of words that go together in groups of three, rather than pairs. Encourage them by pointing out how some have turned into sayings, such as 'lock, stock and barrel'. The group chooses such a saying and mimes it so that other groups can guess what it is. Allow a few minutes preparation, and give help to any group having difficulties eg. Tom, Dick and Harry; Bell, Book and Candle.

Should a group select three things which are not strictly a saying or expression, eg. knife, fork and spoon, do not discourage them. This exercise encourages thinking as well as doing, and develops greater flexibility than working in pairs.

Key	
Focus	*Creativity* ☑ *Skills* ☑ *Insight* ☐
Grouping	*Whole Group* ☐ *2* ☐ *3* ☑ *4* ☐ *5* ☐
Time	*5-10 min* ☐ *10-15 min* ☐ *15-20 min* ☑
Anxiety	*Low* ☐ *Medium* ☑ *High* ☐
Music	*Helpful* ☐ *Not relevant* ☑
R.P.P.	*Useful for Role Play Practice* ☑

GAMES

II: Competitive

9: Fox and Lambs

This game requires quick reactions, so it needs to be explained well; and a practice run may be necessary.

A small cushion or soft ball is needed. One group member is nominated as the fox, and the remainder are lambs. The fox captures lambs by placing the cushion on people's chests. The only way to avoid capture is to stand chest-to-chest with another lamb — but this can only last for a count of three, after which the lambs must run away again!

Development/variations:

(i)   Place mats or cushions around the room. Sheep may not be caught when standing on a mat — but after a count of three they have to move on!

Key	
Focus	*Creativity* ☑ *Skills* ☑ *Insight* ☐
Grouping	*Whole Group* ☑ *2* ☐ *3* ☐ *4* ☐ *5* ☐
Time	*5-10 min* ☐ *10-15 min* ☐ *15-20 min* ☑
Anxiety	*Low* ☑ *Medium* ☐ *High* ☐
Music	*Helpful* ☐ *Not relevant* ☑
R.P.P.	*Useful for Role Play Practice* ☐

GAMES

II: Competitive

10: Stick-in-the-mud

For this game, group members are asked to scatter around the room and attempt to escape being caught by the person who has been chosen to be 'it'. If someone is caught, he/she is said to be 'stuck in the mud' and can only be released by another person crawling through his/her legs. The aim of the individual who is 'it', is to move fast enough that *everyone* is 'stuck in the mud'.

NB: If the group is large, it is advisable for two people to be 'it' simultaneously.

Key	
Focus	*Creativity* ☐ *Skills* ☑ *Insight* ☐
Grouping	*Whole Group* ☑ *2* ☐ *3* ☐ *4* ☐ *5* ☐
Time	*5-10 min* ☐ *10-15 min* ☑ *15-20 min* ☐
Anxiety	*Low* ☑ *Medium* ☐ *High* ☐
Music	*Helpful* ☐ *Not relevant* ☑
R.P.P.	*Useful for Role Play Practice* ☐

GAMES

II: Competitive

11: Off Ground Tig

The object of this game is for group members to avoid being caught by whoever is 'it'. It is an energetic activity, for which it is useful to scatter hoops, cushions or rostras around the room. To avoid being caught, an individual may 'get off the ground', but *only* for a count of three, after which they must move on again.

Development/variations:

(i) Suggest that members work in pairs.

(ii) Put only a few rostras around the room and allow only one person 'off ground' at a time.

Key	
Focus	*Creativity* ☐ *Skills* ☑ *Insight* ☐
Grouping	*Whole Group* ☑ *2* ☐ *3* ☐ *4* ☐ *5* ☐
Time	*5-10 min* ☐ *10-15 min* ☑ *15-20 min* ☐
Anxiety	*Low* ☑ *Medium* ☐ *High* ☐
Music	*Helpful* ☐ *Not relevant* ☑
R.P.P.	*Useful for Role Play Practice* ☐

GAMES

III: Concentration

12: Grandmother's Footsteps

This activity encourages concentration and control.

One member is chosen to be 'grandmother' and stands at one end of the room, facing the wall. The object of the game is to creep slowly towards grandmother, from behind, and to succeed in touching her on the back. Meanwhile, grandmother turns around every few seconds to see if she can see anyone moving. As soon as grandmother begins to turn, everyone should 'freeze', to avoid being disqualified.

The first member to cover the whole length of the room *undetected* becomes grandmother.

Key	
Focus	*Creativity* ☐ *Skills* ☐ *Insight* ☑ ☐
Grouping	*Whole Group* ☑ *2* ☐ *3* ☐ *4* ☐ *5* ☐
Time	*5-10 min* ☐ *10-15 min* ☐ *15-20 min* ☑ ☐
Anxiety	*Low* ☑ *Medium* ☐ *High* ☐
Music	*Helpful* ☐ *Not relevant* ☑
R.P.P.	*Useful for Role Play Practice* ☐

GAMES

III: Concentration

13: What's the time Mr. Wolf?

This game follows the same principle as the previous one, in that one member is chosen to represent the 'wolf' and the remainder of the group creep up behind him. As the group advance, they call "What's the time, Mr. Wolf?" and each time they ask, Mr. Wolf tells them the time. When the group are getting close to him, Mr. Wolf's reply is "12 o'clock and time to eat you up", upon which he chases the group and captures the individual he has chosen for his lunch!

Concentration and quick reactions are required for this game. Whoever gets caught becomes the new Mr. Wolf.

Key	
Focus	*Creativity* ☐ *Skills* ☑ *Insight* ☐
Grouping	*Whole Group* ☑ *2* ☐ *3* ☐ *4* ☐ *5* ☐
Time	*5-10 min* ☐ *10-15 min* ☑ *15-20 min* ☐
Anxiety	*Low* ☑ *Medium* ☐ *High* ☐
Music	*Helpful* ☐ *Not relevant* ☑
R.P.P.	*Useful for Role Play Practice* ☐

GAMES

IV: Guessing/Memory

14: I Spy

Usually, the game is played sitting in a circle. Its level can be adapted to the abilities of the group.

One member begins:

"I spy with my little eye something beginning with . . . (a letter of the alphabet)."

The rest of the group then attempt to guess what object or person in the room it may be. Whoever guesses the word correctly has the next turn at 'I Spy'.

Development/variations:

Encourage the group to make up variations eg. giving the *last* letter of a word as the clue; miming the letter, or modifying ground rules to make the clues easier or harder.

Key	
Focus	*Creativity* ☐ *Skills* ☐ *Insight* ☐
Grouping	*Whole Group* ☑ *2* ☐ *3* ☐ *4* ☐ *5* ☐
Time	*5-10 min* ☐ *10-15 min* ☑ *15-20 min* ☐
Anxiety	*Low* ☑ *Medium* ☐ *High* ☐
Music	*Helpful* ☐ *Not relevant* ☑
R.P.P.	*Useful for Role Play Practice* ☑

IV: Guessing/Memory

15: Holiday Shopping

This is a very useful memory game and can also be fun! The leader should first explain the procedure carefully:

One member begins with "I went on holiday to . . . and I bought . . ." The next member of the group repeats the above statement, but adds a further item of shopping eg. I went to Greece and I bought olives (and worry beads).

The third member adds yet another item of shopping; and each item must be related to the chosen country.

Development/variations:
(i)   Use different countries and different objects each time.
(ii) Suggest buying something very 'silly' from each country.
(iii) Have country and item starting with the same letter, eg. a dog from Denmark.

Key	
Focus	*Creativity* ☐ *Skills* ☑ *Insight* ☐
Grouping	*Whole Group* ☑ *2* ☐ *3* ☐ *4* ☐ *5* ☐
Time	*5-10 min* ☐ *10-15 min* ☑ *15-20 min* ☑
Anxiety	*Low* ☑ *Medium* ☐ *High* ☐
Music	*Helpful* ☐ *Not relevant* ☑
R.P.P.	*Useful for Role Play Practice* ☑

IV: Guessing/Memory

16: The Air Balloon

Out of the whole group, four members are asked to volunteer to go up in a hot air balloon. These four assume the roles of a famous surgeon, a prime minister, a bishop and an artist.

Explain to these four that their air balloon is regrettably losing height fast, and that all will perish unless one of them nobly agrees to jump out. It is then up to each passenger to present a good argument for staying in the balloon!

When all four arguments have been put forward, the remainder of the group should be invited to judge whose cases were the most convincing and why.

Key	
Focus	*Creativity* ☐ *Skills* ☑ *Insight* ☑
Grouping	*Whole Group* ☑ *2* ☐ *3* ☐ *4* ☐ *5* ☐
Time	*5-10 min* ☐ *10-15 min* ☐ *15-20 min* ☑
Anxiety	*Low* ☐ *Medium* ☐ *High* ☑
Music	*Helpful* ☐ *Not relevant* ☑
R.P.P.	*Useful for Role Play Practice* ☑

GAMES

IV: Guessing/Memory

17: Words in Mood

First, the whole group selects a saying or jingle, eg. "Every nice girl loves a sailor".

The leader prepares before the session a list of 'feeling' adverbs eg. happily, regally, furiously, timidly.

Next, members divide themselves into small groups from each of which a representative goes to the leader to be told one 'feeling'. These representatives say the chosen phrase with that particular feeling, and the teams attempt to guess the adverb which has been demonstrated.

As soon as one adverb has been guessed, another team member is given another adverb to convey. The team who guess *all* the chosen adverbs the quickest, wins. This is helped greatly by clear communication.

Key	
Focus	*Creativity* ☑ *Skills* ☑ *Insight* ☐
Grouping	*Whole Group* ☑ *2* ☐ *3* ☐ *4* ☑ *5* ☑
Time	*5-10 min* ☐ *10-15 min* ☑ *15-20 min* ☑
Anxiety	*Low* ☐ *Medium* ☑ *High* ☐
Music	*Helpful* ☐ *Not relevant* ☑
R.P.P.	*Useful for Role Play Practice* ☑

GAMES

V: Conceptual

18: Change the Baton

Ask the group to sit in a circle and give them a baton or stick to pass round.

The object of the game is for each member to use the baton to represent an object, and for the rest of the group to guess what this is eg. wooden spoon; flute; something sporting.

If it proves difficult to guess what a person's 'object' is, then he or she should be encouraged to mime in greater detail.

Development/variations:
(i) Suggest that the baton be used to represent something very small/very large.
(ii) Suggest that it be used for something that involves another person, or animal.

Key	
Focus	*Creativity* ☑ *Skills* ☑ *Insight* ☐
Grouping	*Whole Group* ☑ *2* ☐ *3* ☐ *4* ☐ *5* ☐
Time	*5-10 min* ☐ *10-15 min* ☐ *15-20 min* ☑
Anxiety	*Low* ☑ *Medium* ☐ *High* ☐
Music	*Helpful* ☐ *Not relevant* ☑
R.P.P.	*Useful for Role Play Practice* ☐

GAMES

V: Conceptual

19: Change the Object

For this activity, it is best if the group sits in a circle. It may be necessary for the leader to demonstrate how the game should be played. Members should be encouraged to be as original and imaginative as possible.

A cushion, chair or other substantial object should be placed in the centre of the circle, and each member in turn is invited to use that object to represent something else eg. a TV set; a mixing bowl; a shower.

Other members of the group must guess the object being 'mimed'.

Development/variations:
(i)   The group may divide into pairs who work on, or with, the object together.
(ii)   It may be suggested that each 'object' should be either 'from the kitchen' etc. or actually *alive*.

Key	
Focus	*Creativity* ☑ *Skills* ☑ *Insight* ☐
Grouping	*Whole Group* ☑ *2* ☐ *3* ☐ *4* ☐ *5* ☐
Time	*5-10 min* ☐ *10-15 min* ☑ *15-20 min* ☐
Anxiety	*Low* ☑ *Medium* ☐ *High* ☐
Music	*Helpful* ☐ *Not relevant* ☑
R.P.P.	*Useful for Role Play Practice* ☐

GAMES

V: Conceptual

20: Mime the Object

Arrange group members in a circle, and mime an object for them. Once people have guessed what that object is, 'hand it' to someone and instruct him or her to "change it into something else". The object can be passed around the whole circle, being changed by each individual in turn, and must be given and taken as if it were a real object, with clear accurate mime and not just gesture.

NB: Do not let this activity become a competition for the cleverest mime.

Key	
Focus	*Creativity* ☑ *Skills* ☑ *Insight* ☐
Grouping	*Whole Group* ☑ *2* ☐ *3* ☐ *4* ☐ *5* ☐
Time	*5-10 min* ☐ *10-15 min* ☑ *15-20 min* ☐
Anxiety	*Low* ☑ *Medium* ☐ *High* ☐
Music	*Helpful* ☐ *Not relevant* ☑
R.P.P.	*Useful for Role Play Practice* ☐

GAMES

V: Conceptual

21: The Group in Unison

For this activity, select two members to assist the leader as 'monitors', to see that the rest of the group are carrying out their instructions in unison.

First, establish some ground rules and explain the game clearly eg. once the game starts, it must be seen through to a conclusion and there should be no unnecessary talking apart from what is needed in the task.

Ask individuals to carry out a list of four instructions, then to repeat these in perfect unison with a partner, then to repeat them in fours and finally all together. If any activity is not perfectly synchronised, the sequence must be repeated.

Examples: March on the spot 10 times, then touch the floor, then sing the first verse of Twinkle Twinkle Little Star, and finally complete the sentence "Living is . . . " (The latter gives rise to much group discussion).

Key	
Focus	*Creativity* ☐ *Skills* ☑ *Insight* ☑
Grouping	*Whole Group* ☑ *2* ☑ *3* ☐ *4* ☑ *5* ☐
Time	*5-10 min* ☐ *10-15 min* ☐ *15-20 min* ☑
Anxiety	*Low* ☐ *Medium* ☐ *High* ☑
Music	*Helpful* ☐ *Not relevant* ☑
R.P.P.	*Useful for Role Play Practice* ☐

GAMES

V: Conceptual

22: Similarities and Differences

This activity develops a clearer sense of 'self and other'. It is advisable to warm up the group physically before the game (eg. warm ups 12, 13 or 16).

Ask members to scatter around the room and 'freeze'.

Then explain that they may each choose to be either a swan, a goose or a penguin and encourage them to move around the room using their bodies, limbs and heads as if they are those birds. Allow up to 2 minutes for this, after which the swans, geese and penguins should all join forces in three groups and move *together* as those birds. Encourage the groups to check that they are matched correctly.

Other groupings may be used eg. robin/sparrow/wren; giraffe/camel/llama; rhinoceros/hippopotamus/elephant.

Accuracy of movement should be encouraged.

Development/variations:
(i)   Divide into eg. fox, wolf and hunting dog; and add *sounds* to movements.
(ii) Discuss essential differences and what groups may have in common.

Key	
Focus	*Creativity* ☑ *Skills* ☐ *Insight* ☐
Grouping	*Whole Group* ☑ *2* ☐ *3* ☐ *4* ☐ *5* ☑
Time	*5-10 min* ☐ *10-15 min* ☐ *15-20 min* ☑
Anxiety	*Low* ☐ *Medium* ☑ *High* ☑
Music	*Helpful* ☐ *Not relevant* ☑
R.P.P.	*Useful for Role Play Practice* ☑

V: Conceptual

23: Group Similarities and Differences

Name warm ups are ideal before this game eg. 2, 3 and 5.

Explain to the group that members should move around the room chanting the initial letter of their name — first very quietly, but gradually getting louder and louder, until the letters are being shouted as loud as possible. The object of the exercise is to find others whose names begin with the same letter: some will find they make a group, others may form pairs, while a few may find that they are alone. The latter should link up with other 'solitary letters' and find *different* ways in which they may be similar, eg. birthdays, colour of eyes.

Each of the groups should try to find five things they have in common, and relate these to the whole group at the end of the activity.

Development/variations:
(i)   The similarities which groups identify may be *mimed* rather than verbalised to the whole group.
(ii) Similarities may be *chanted* in an improvised rhythm, with movement.

Key	
Focus	*Creativity* ☑ *Skills* ☑ *Insight* ☐
Grouping	*Whole Group* ☑ *2* ☑ *3* ☑ *4* ☑ *5* ☑
Time	*5-10 min* ☑ *10-15 min* ☐ *15-20 min* ☐
Anxiety	*Low* ☐ *Medium* ☑ *High* ☐
Music	*Helpful* ☐ *Not relevant* ☑
R.P.P.	*Useful for Role Play Practice* ☑

V: Conceptual

24: Killer Wink

This game has the advantages of being exciting and requiring a lot of concentrating, while the group remains physically static.

It makes a very good warm up itself for a 'who dunnit' piece of drama work. Likewise, various detective board games such as Cluedo may be used in preparation for the invitation: "Now, lets make up our *own* detective story".

Ask the group to sit in a circle and tell one volunteer — the detective — to turn his or her back or leave the room briefly. Meanwhile, the group must decide who will play the murderer. The detective's task is to identify this person.

On the arrival of the detective, the murderer may begin to 'kill' the victims — this is done simply by winking at them when the detective is not looking. Groups tend to enjoy playing 'Killer Wink' repeatedly, and detective skills can be improved.

Key	
Focus	*Creativity* ☑ *Skills* ☑ *Insight* ☐
Grouping	*Whole Group* ☑ *2* ☐ *3* ☐ *4* ☐ *5* ☐
Time	*5-10 min* ☐ *10-15 min* ☑ *15-20 min* ☐
Anxiety	*Low* ☑ *Medium* ☐ *High* ☐
Music	*Helpful* ☐ *Not relevant* ☑
R.P.P.	*Useful for Role Play Practice* ☐

VI: Community

25: Build a Community

The leader is advised to have all necessary materials to hand before this activity.

Arrange the groups seated around tables and explain that a specific amount of time will be allowed (perhaps 20-30 mins) to co-operate in building up a community or village. This game naturally requires both negotiation and eventual agreement.

Materials provided may include some, or all, of the following: clay or sand; newspaper; scissors; glue; string; and perhaps extras such as shells, stones, toy animals and people.

Development/variations:

To make the activity more challenging, the group may be instructed that *verbal* communication is not allowed.

Key	
Focus	*Creativity* ☑ *Skills* ☑ *Insight* ☑
Grouping	*Whole Group* ☑ *2* ☐ *3* ☐ *4* ☐ *5* ☑
Time	*5-10 min* ☐ *10-15 min* ☑ *15-20 min* ☑
Anxiety	*Low* ☐ *Medium* ☐ *High* ☑
Music	*Helpful* ☐ *Not relevant* ☑
R.P.P.	*Useful for Role Play Practice* ☑

VI: Community

26: Survival

For this game, the group is divided into two, with each half starting at opposite ends of the room.

The leader explains what different parts of the room represent. One group is living on cultivated land with food and crops. The other is in a deep forest which may hide treasure. There is a fast-flowing river in between the two. Explain that the two groups speak different languages and do not understand each other.

Both groups have to survive and somehow co-exist. They may or may not choose to *try* to communicate.

Materials required for this imaginative game include: cardboard boxes, newspapers, glue and cellotape.

NB: A time limit must be set for this absorbing game (perhaps 20-45 minutes, depending on the group).

Key	
Focus	*Creativity* ☑ *Skills* ☑ *Insight* ☑
Grouping	*Whole Group* ☑ *2* ☐ *3* ☐ *4* ☐ *5* ☑
Time	*5-10 min* ☐ *10-15 min* ☐ *15-20 min* ☑
Anxiety	*Low* ☐ *Medium* ☐ *High* ☑
Music	*Helpful* ☐ *Not relevant* ☑
R.P.P.	*Useful for Role Play Practice* ☑

GAMES

VI: Community

27: Planning Escape

This activity can be used as a 'bridge' in working towards improvisation. Very clear instructions should be given. The group imagines they are trapped in a hut in the middle of a large forest, that food is running out, and to stay there is becoming dangerous.

To reach freedom it will be necessary to tackle the following obstacles:
(i)   break out of the hut
(ii)   climb a 20ft barricade
(iii)   negotiate a barbed wire fence
(iv)   cross a river
(v)   penetrate some deep forest
(vi)   travel through a malarial swamp

Discussion should centre around what *three things* would be most useful to enable the group to escape. Members may contribute a variety of ideas, but magic words, laser beams and helicopters etc. are not permitted!

Key	
Focus	*Creativity* ☑ *Skills* ☑ *Insight* ☑
Grouping	*Whole Group* ☐ *2* ☐ *3* ☐ *4* ☐ *5* ☑
Time	*5-10 min* ☐ *10-15 min* ☐ *15-20 min* ☑
Anxiety	*Low* ☐ *Medium* ☐ *High* ☑
Music	*Helpful* ☐ *Not relevant* ☑
R.P.P.	*Useful for Role Play Practice* ☑

VI: Community

28: Enacting Escape

This game of make-believe is played as in the previous exercise, 'Planning Escape'.

Once the group has discussed possible strategies for escape and some collective decisions have been made, chairs and other large pieces of equipment can be used to construct the obstacles. Group members then enact the escape journey, with as great a sense of realism as possible.

After the escapes have been concluded, the groups may wish to combine in order to share their experiences:

Did anyone get left behind?

What were the most difficult problems?

Could easier solutions have been found?

What would each person most like when freedom was achieved?

Key	
Focus	*Creativity* ☑ *Skills* ☑ *Insight* ☑
Grouping	*Whole Group* ☐ *2* ☐ *3* ☐ *4* ☐ *5* ☑
Time	*5-10 min* ☐ *10-15 min* ☐ *15-20 min* ☑
Anxiety	*Low* ☐ *Medium* ☐ *High* ☑
Music	*Helpful* ☐ *Not relevant* ☑
R.P.P.	*Useful for Role Play Practice* ☑

VI: Community

29: Depicting Escape

For this variation on the escape theme, large pieces of paper, felt tip pens and crayons are required.

The game is begun as in No. 27 'Planning Escape'.

Once the journey and other details have been discussed in small groups, large pieces of paper should be provided for each to draw a group map charting the planned escape. The vegetation and fauna encountered on the route may also be drawn and coloured.

At the end of this game, groups may wish to compare maps and discuss the decisions they took.

Development/variations:
(i)   Design a similar escape from a prison.

Key	
Focus	*Creativity* ☑ *Skills* ☐ *Insight* ☑
Grouping	*Whole Group* ☑ *2* ☐ *3* ☐ *4* ☐ *5* ☑
Time	*5-10 min* ☐ *10-15 min* ☐ *15-20 min* ☑
Anxiety	*Low* ☐ *Medium* ☑ *High* ☑
Music	*Helpful* ☐ *Not relevant* ☑
R.P.P.	*Useful for Role Play Practice* ☐

GAMES

VI: Community

30: An Escape Remembered

The object of this game of make-believe is for individuals to imagine that they achieved their daring and difficult escape many, many years ago.

The activity begins as in No. 27, 'Planning Escape'. When the essential planning and decision-making have been achieved, members are invited to close their eyes and imagine themselves a generation older. It may be helpful for the leader to facilitate the story-telling by saying: "Tell your children, how, many, many years ago . . ."

Development/variations:

Design a similar escape from captivity on a pirate ship.

Key	
Focus	*Creativity* ☐ *Skills* ☐ *Insight* ☑
Grouping	*Whole Group* ☑ *2* ☐ *3* ☐ *4* ☐ *5* ☑
Time	*5-10 min* ☐ *10-15 min* ☑ *15-20 min* ☑
Anxiety	*Low* ☐ *Medium* ☐ *High* ☑
Music	*Helpful* ☐ *Not relevant* ☑
R.P.P.	*Useful for Role Play Practice* ☐

IMPROVISATION AND ROLE PLAY

I: Role Play Preparation

1: Ways of Walking

In role play preparation, participants are helped to differentiate their movements and increase their range of voice usage.

Use exercise 20 as a warm up for this activity.

The leader invites the group to consider and demonstrate the following: "How do I walk if . . .

I am old; I have just learned to walk; I am wearing high-heeled shoes; I am wearing Wellington boots; I am wearing 'flip-flops'; I am wearing new shoes; I am pushing a pram; I am carrying heavy baskets; I have a strong dog on a lead?"

"How do I walk . . .

in mud; in gravel; on ice; in treacle; through Autumn leaves; through shallow water?"

Key	
Focus	*Creativity* ☑ *Skills* ☐ *Insight* ☑
Grouping	*Whole Group* ☑ *2* ☐ *3* ☐ *4* ☐ *5* ☐
Time	*5-10 min* ☑ *10-15 min* ☑ *15-20 min* ☑
Anxiety	*Low* ☑ *Medium* ☐ *High* ☐
Music	*Helpful* ☐ *Not relevant* ☑
R.P.P.	*Useful for Role Play Practice* ☑

IMPROVISATION AND ROLE PLAY

I: Role Play Preparation

2: Ways of Sitting

This activity may be introduced in the same way as the previous exercise. Ask group members to sit on chairs, in a circle, and to consider the many different ways in which people sit.

Let them experiment and see if they can simulate the following: "How might I sit if . . .

I was nervous at an interview; I wanted to avoid people talking to me; I was trying to stop myself laughing; I was worried about seeing the doctor; I was anxious about an injection; I was nodding off to sleep; I was at a demonstration and was refusing to be moved?"

Key	
Focus	*Creativity* ☑ *Skills* ☐ *Insight* ☑
Grouping	*Whole Group* ☑ *2* ☐ *3* ☐ *4* ☐ *5* ☐
Time	*5-10 min* ☑ *10-15 min* ☐ *15-20 min* ☑
Anxiety	*Low* ☑ *Medium* ☐ *High* ☐
Music	*Helpful* ☐ *Not relevant* ☑
R.P.P.	*Useful for Role Play Practice* ☑

IMPROVISATION
AND ROLE PLAY

I: Role Play Preparation

3: Feelings

Prepare in advance a set of 'feelings' cards as described in
Section I, page 28.

Give each group member a card and encourage them to
consider and attempt to simulate the details of eg. an *angry*
person; a *loving* person; a *conceited* person.

It may prove helpful to discuss with individuals such details as
what age they are portraying, what they are wearing, where
they are etc.

This, and many of the warm-up exercises for voice and body,
are useful introductions to role play. Variations on this type of
activity may help to develop a wider repertoire in voice and body
use, responding to varying stimuli and changing roles.

Key	
Focus	*Creativity* ☑ *Skills* ☐ *Insight* ☑
Grouping	*Whole Group* ☑ *2* ☐ *3* ☐ *4* ☐ *5* ☐
Time	*5-10 min* ☐ *10-15 min* ☑ *15-20 min* ☑
Anxiety	*Low* ☐ *Medium* ☑ *High* ☐
Music	*Helpful* ☐ *Not relevant* ☑
R.P.P.	*Useful for Role Play Practice* ☑

IMPROVISATION AND ROLE PLAY

I: Role Play Preparation

4: Becoming a Character

As in exercise 3, this activity uses ready-prepared 'feeling' cards. (See Warm Ups No. 32).

Each member of the group picks a card from the pile and becomes a *character* with that feeling eg. an angry postman; a tired teacher; an energetic vicar; an irritated carpenter.

After some practice, several of the characters may be brought together to evolve and improvise a scene. After a specified time, this scene may be shown to other group members.

Key	
Focus	*Creativity* ☑ *Skills* ☐ *Insight* ☑
Grouping	*Whole Group* ☑ *2* ☐ *3* ☑ *4* ☑ *5* ☐
Time	*5-10 min* ☐ *10-15 min* ☑ *15-20 min* ☑
Anxiety	*Low* ☐ *Medium* ☑ *High* ☐
Music	*Helpful* ☐ *Not relevant* ☑
R.P.P.	*Useful for Role Play Practice* ☑

IMPROVISATION AND ROLE PLAY

I: Role Play Preparation

5: *The Sea, in Movement*

For this activity, the leader initiates discussion on the theme of the sea, encouraging the identification of images rather than events (ie. how people picture the sea in colours, sensations and movement, rather than what may have happened on a trip to the sea-side).

Using selected pieces of music (eg. Fingal's Cave) movements and sequences can then be developed. These may begin as gentle warm up movements but expanding into contrasting movements using the whole body. Small sub-groups may concentrate on individual movements which can then be brought together to highlight contrasts eg. small waves; big waves; enormous breakers.

All of these contributions can finally be woven together into a 'piece' which evokes the sea through movement.

Development/variations:

A sea poem such as Sea Fever or The Ancient Mariner may be used instead of music, to create an atmosphere.

Key	
Focus	*Creativity* ☑ *Skills* ☐ *Insight* ☑
Grouping	*Whole Group* ☑ *2* ☑ *3* ☑ *4* ☑ *5* ☑
Time	*5-10 min* ☑ *10-15 min* ☑ *15-20 min* ☑
Anxiety	*Low* ☑ *Medium* ☑ *High* ☐
Music	*Helpful* ☑ *Not relevant* ☐
R.P.P.	*Useful for Role Play Practice* ☐

IMPROVISATION AND ROLE PLAY

I: Role Play Preparation

6: What is in the Sea

Following a physical warm up, members are encouraged to develop ideas about what is in and under the sea. Pictures and posters are valuable props for this activity.

Having identified some of the groups of creatures, for example, members may choose which type they will represent in movement, as individuals eg. crabs, sword fish, sea slugs, dolphins, sea anemones.

Then they may be invited to form pairs or threes and move as seaweed, octopuses etc. Small groups may represent shoals of tiny fish which move in and out of the coral reef (formed by other group members). Finally, the whole range of movements may be brought together, using music or sound effects to create an underwater scene.

Key	
Focus	*Creativity* ☑ *Skills* ☐ *Insight* ☑
Grouping	*Whole Group* ☑ *2* ☐ *3* ☑ *4* ☑ *5* ☐
Time	*5-10 min* ☑ *10-15 min* ☑ *15-20 min* ☑
Anxiety	*Low* ☐ *Medium* ☑ *High* ☐
Music	*Helpful* ☑ *Not relevant* ☐
R.P.P.	*Useful for Role Play Practice* ☐

IMPROVISATION AND ROLE PLAY

I: Role Play Preparation

7: At the Sea-side

The leader initiates discussion of group members' memories or impressions of the sea-side. These may be good or bad: picnics, donkey rides, Punch and Judy, eating rock; being stung, getting lost, bossy landladies.

Improvisation of scenes from people's lives can then be encouraged, based upon a sea-side scene, with titles such as: "On the pier . . .".

Development/variations:
(i)   Invite the group to improvise funny/risqué scenes eg. crabs and bottoms.
(ii) Introduce an element of suspense by beginning "A mystery has occurred at this little sea-side town. Is it smuggling? Is it a detective story? Has a body been washed up on the beach? Choose something like this, and improvise the story."

Key	
Focus	*Creativity* ☑ *Skills* ☑ *Insight* ☑
Grouping	*Whole Group* ☑ *2* ☑ *3* ☑ *4* ☑ *5* ☑
Time	*5-10 min* ☐ *10-15 min* ☑ *15-20 min* ☑
Anxiety	*Low* ☐ *Medium* ☑ *High* ☐
Music	*Helpful* ☑ *Not relevant* ☐
R.P.P.	*Useful for Role Play Practice* ☑

IMPROVISATION AND ROLE PLAY

I: Role Play Preparation

8: Sea-farers

This activity may either develop into a 'fun' scene, not unlike Gilbert and Sullivan, or it may lead to more serious exploration of the real horrors of pirate exploits, and of the opposing forces of law and order.

After a vocal warm up, the leader involves the group in singing pirate songs and shanties, recounting pirate adventures and discussion of where and what hidden treasure may be sought in an *improvised* story.

The story can evolve as the whole group, or smaller groups of about 5, go to sea on a plundering expedition. Members must first discuss who will take various roles, such as captain, where they are sailing, where they were moored last night etc.

Key	
Focus	*Creativity* ☑ *Skills* ☐ *Insight* ☑
Grouping	*Whole Group* ☑ *2* ☑ *3* ☑ *4* ☑ *5* ☑
Time	*5-10 min* ☐ *10-15 min* ☑ *15-20 min* ☑
Anxiety	*Low* ☐ *Medium* ☑ *High* ☐
Music	*Helpful* ☑ *Not relevant* ☐
R.P.P.	*Useful for Role Play Practice* ☑

IMPROVISATION AND ROLE PLAY

I: Role Play Preparation

9: Sea Stories

The leader is advised to do some preparatory research on sea stories before introducing this topic to the group. Members are encouraged to re-tell and re-enact ancient stories, myths and legends such as 'The Boy on the Dolphin' or a Poseidon story (Neptune).

Appropriate sound effects and/or music can be helpful here.

Either the whole group may co-operate to create a story, or smaller groups may choose to contribute one scene each.

Development/variations:

(i)   The group can improvise their own ancient sea legend. Adequate time must be allowed for this to evolve.

(ii) Improvisation may be developed on the themes of 'Sea Gods' or 'Sea Devils', perhaps using home made masks prepared in a previous session.

Key	
Focus	*Creativity* ☑ *Skills* ☐ *Insight* ☑
Grouping	*Whole Group* ☑ *2* ☐ *3* ☐ *4* ☐ *5* ☑
Time	*5-10 min* ☐ *10-15 min* ☑ *15-20 min* ☑
Anxiety	*Low* ☐ *Medium* ☑ *High* ☐
Music	*Helpful* ☑ *Not relevant* ☐
R.P.P.	*Useful for Role Play Practice* ☑

IMPROVISATION AND ROLE PLAY

I: Role Play Preparation

10: The Commercial

This activity starts with a general discussion about advertising, with members commenting on what commercials they do and do not like. The group can be asked, for example, if they actually remember commercials when they are out shopping.

A preliminary game can be set up, to see if people can remember or guess which tunes or jingles 'belong' to which products, and vice versa.

Divide into small groups: members try enacting, *without words*, a commercial for the other groups to guess.

Development/variations:
(i)   Commercials may be enacted *with* words.
(ii) New commercials may be thought up, to sell a known product.
(iii) Ridiculous commercials may be made up, to sell things (eg. an elephant) which would not normally be advertised.

Key	
Focus	*Creativity* ☑ *Skills* ☑ *Insight* ☑
Grouping	*Whole Group* ☑ *2* ☑ *3* ☑ *4* ☑ *5* ☑
Time	*5-10 min* ☐ *10-15 min* ☑ *15-20 min* ☑
Anxiety	*Low* ☐ *Medium* ☑ *High* ☐
Music	*Helpful* ☑ *Not relevant* ☐
R.P.P.	*Useful for Role Play Practice* ☑

IMPROVISATION AND ROLE PLAY

I: Role Play Preparation

11: TV Scenes

This activity is best developed from an initial discussion of group members' favourite TV programmes and TV dramas. There may be wide variation in what people watch regularly and what individuals do and do not like.

The aim of enacting TV scenes is to encourage members to 'get inside' the roles they play — unless they are specifically invited to present a caricature. If the leader wishes the group to 'send up' a programme or TV drama, then this should be made clear at the outset.

Some groups may require warming up to the idea of presenting a realistic 'character'.

A specific time limit, eg. 3 minutes, must be set for each scene.

Development/variations:
(i)   Prepare role cards beforehand, based upon TV characters.
(ii) Invite members to enact what may happen 'in next week's episode'.

Key	
Focus	*Creativity* ☑ *Skills* ☑ *Insight* ☑
Grouping	*Whole Group* ☑ *2* ☑ *3* ☑ *4* ☑ *5* ☑
Time	*5-10 min* ☐ *10-15 min* ☑ *15-20 min* ☑
Anxiety	*Low* ☐ *Medium* ☑ *High* ☐
Music	*Helpful* ☐ *Not relevant* ☑
R.P.P.	*Useful for Role Play Practice* ☑

IMPROVISATION AND ROLE PLAY

I: Role Play Preparation

12: Famous People Party

This activity can be introduced through general discussion of what famous people the group have seen/like/dislike/long to meet etc.

A helpful warm up involves suggesting that members walk around the room *as if* they were . . .

A Prime Minister making a speech

The Queen greeting people

An actor playing Hamlet

The leader asks each member to think of a famous person; slowly 'become' that person; and then interact with other famous people at an imaginary party. Each VIP can be formally introduced to the other guests.

Development/variations:

Unlikely meetings may be arranged eg. Attila the Hun and Queen Victoria.

Key	
Focus	*Creativity* ☑ *Skills* ☑ *Insight* ☑
Grouping	*Whole Group* ☑ *2* ☐ *3* ☐ *4* ☐ *5* ☐
Time	*5-10 min* ☐ *10-15 min* ☑ *15-20 min* ☑
Anxiety	*Low* ☐ *Medium* ☑ *High* ☐
Music	*Helpful* ☑ *Not relevant* ☐
R.P.P.	*Useful for Role Play Practice* ☑

IMPROVISATION AND ROLE PLAY

II: Improvisation

13: Opening Lines

NB: Bearing in mind that people may take time to learn to improvise and at first may only be able to sustain a character or scene very briefly, the scope and time allowed for this exercise should be increased very gradually.

For this activity, the leader gives each small group an opening line. These can be written on role cards, or given verbally. A time limit *must* be set for groups to develop dramatic improvisation *starting* with the opening lines supplied. It is helpful to warn members when the time is running out.

Examples:
(i) Bernadette had just settled down in front of a warm fire with a good book when . . .
(ii) Peter walked briskly down the street, eager to get home, and . . .
(iii) The policeman tried the door handle of the darkened terraced house and . . .
(iv) James and Polly were laughing as they walked home from the party: suddenly . . .

Key	
Focus	*Creativity* ☑ *Skills* ☐ *Insight* ☑
Grouping	*Whole Group* ☐ *2* ☐ *3* ☑ *4* ☑ *5* ☐
Time	*5-10 min* ☐ *10-15 min* ☑ *15-20 min* ☑
Anxiety	*Low* ☐ *Medium* ☑ *High* ☐
Music	*Helpful* ☐ *Not relevant* ☑
R.P.P.	*Useful for Role Play Practice* ☑

II: Improvisation

14: Ending Lines

This exercise can be approached similarly to the previous improvisation, 'Opening Lines'. *Ending* lines are supplied for small groups to create the imaginary situation leading up to them. These may be given verbally, or written on cards which the leader has prepared before the session. A time limit for this exercise is essential, since members tend to discuss their scenes in detail but are slow to get round to acting them!

Examples:
(i)   "Well that", said the Judge, "will be a lesson to you all."
(ii) "Tomorrow is another day," she whispered to herself as she dropped off to sleep.
(iii) "Cornflakes? Cornflakes? You must be out of your mind!"

Key	
Focus	*Creativity* ☑ *Skills* ☐ *Insight* ☑
Grouping	*Whole Group* ☐ *2* ☐ *3* ☑ *4* ☑ *5* ☐
Time	*5-10 min* ☐ *10-15 min* ☑ *15-20 min* ☑
Anxiety	*Low* ☐ *Medium* ☑ *High* ☐
Music	*Helpful* ☐ *Not relevant* ☑
R.P.P.	*Useful for Role Play Practice* ☑

IMPROVISATION AND ROLE PLAY

II: Improvisation

15: Incidents

The leader sets a scene for group members, evoking plenty of atmosphere. Within the scene described, an 'incident' occurs.

Each small group is asked to improvise their own incident, show it to other group members, and then a whole group discussion develops when all of the improvisations have been seen.

Example:

"It is now ten o'clock and a fine drizzle of rain has started. There is a small queue of people standing outside the fish and chip van. Suddenly . . .

(i) there is a loud noise

(ii) the sound of a police siren is heard

(iii) there is a horrifying screech of brakes.

Key	
Focus	*Creativity* ☑ *Skills* ☑ *Insight* ☑
Grouping	*Whole Group* ☐ *2* ☑ *3* ☑ *4* ☑ *5* ☑
Time	*5-10 min* ☐ *10-15 min* ☑ *15-20 min* ☑
Anxiety	*Low* ☑ *Medium* ☐ *High* ☐
Music	*Helpful* ☐ *Not relevant* ☑
R.P.P.	*Useful for Role Play Practice* ☑

IMPROVISATION AND ROLE PLAY

II: Improvisation

16: Newspapers

This activity requires a large variety of newspapers.

Before the group session, headlines are cut out and pasted on card.

During the session, small groups may each be given a headline upon which to base an improvisation. This should be a make-believe story or scenario.

When each group has developed an improvisation, the results may be shared with the whole group.

NB: Competitiveness should be discouraged. This activity is intended to develop creative sharing.

Key	
Focus	*Creativity* ☑ *Skills* ☐ *Insight* ☑
Grouping	*Whole Group* ☐ *2* ☐ *3* ☐ *4* ☑ *5* ☑
Time	*5-10 min* ☐ *10-15 min* ☑ *15-20 min* ☑
Anxiety	*Low* ☑ *Medium* ☐ *High* ☐
Music	*Helpful* ☐ *Not relevant* ☑
R.P.P.	*Useful for Role Play Practice* ☑

IMPROVISATION AND ROLE PLAY

II: Improvisation

17: Current Affairs

As for exercise 15, obtain in advance a variety of newspapers. Cut out stories from these, with the endings removed eg. trials, summit talks, management/union meetings, marches, royal visits.

Each small group is given a story and has to improvise their own ending. The scenes should be described for them in plenty of detail; some people may need more information than others before they feel confident about creating their own story ending.

The finished products may be discussed by the whole group at the end, if the leader feels this would be constructive.

Key	
Focus	*Creativity* ☑ *Skills* ☑ *Insight* ☑
Grouping	*Whole Group* ☐ *2* ☐ *3* ☐ *4* ☑ *5* ☑
Time	*5-10 min* ☐ *10-15 min* ☑ *15-20 min* ☑
Anxiety	*Low* ☑ *Medium* ☐ *High* ☐
Music	*Helpful* ☐ *Not relevant* ☑
R.P.P.	*Useful for Role Play Practice* ☑

IMPROVISATION AND ROLE PLAY

II: Improvisation

18: The Park Bench

Before the session the leader prepares sets of role cards related to imaginary scenes. The group is divided into three and each small group is asked to act their scene as convincingly as possible, improvising conversations etc.

Example:
Characters: A smartly dressed man sitting quietly reading a newspaper; a tramp; a lady walking a dog.
Scene: A park bench on a sunny afternoon.
Action: The tramp comes up and decides to ask the man for some money. The lady passes by and joins in the conversation.

Development/variations:
> The scene itself can be described in great detail, but the group is asked to create their *own* characters.

Key	
Focus	*Creativity* ☑ *Skills* ☑ *Insight* ☑
Grouping	*Whole Group* ☐ *2* ☐ *3* ☑ *4* ☐ *5* ☐
Time	*5-10 min* ☐ *10-15 min* ☑ *15-20 min* ☑
Anxiety	*Low* ☐ *Medium* ☑ *High* ☐
Music	*Helpful* ☐ *Not relevant* ☑
R.P.P.	*Useful for Role Play Practice* ☑

IMPROVISATION AND ROLE PLAY

II: Improvisation

19: The Old House

In this exercise, group members are encouraged to listen to and then improvise upon, the following situation:

Characters: Three people are involved. (They know each other/they do not know each other).

Scene: The old house is surrounded by trees. Ivy is growing round the windows and there are some tiles missing from the roof. The drive is unkempt and no-one has pruned the roses for a long time. The large gate, off its hinges, is propped open. The path to the goldfish pond appears untrodden.

Action: Three people find themselves walking together up the drive to the old house . . . and . . .

Key	
Focus	*Creativity* ☑ *Skills* ☐ *Insight* ☑
Grouping	*Whole Group* ☐ *2* ☐ *3* ☑ *4* ☐ *5* ☐
Time	*5-10 min* ☐ *10-15 min* ☑ *15-20 min* ☑
Anxiety	*Low* ☐ *Medium* ☑ *High* ☐
Music	*Helpful* ☐ *Not relevant* ☑
R.P.P.	*Useful for Role Play Practice* ☑

IMPROVISATION AND ROLE PLAY

II: Improvisation

20: The Meeting

The following scene is presented to members for improvisation in groups of three. The varied interpretations can be seen by the rest of the group, at the end of the session, if this sharing is likely to be productive.

Characters: An elderly gentleman wearing a deerstalker; a young woman with a placard (decide what is written upon it); a traffic warden.

Scene: A street in a large city.

Action: These three people meet. What happens when they do?

Development/variations:

The scene may deliberately be developed as a comedy; or on another occasion as a classical tragedy.

Key	
Focus	*Creativity* ☑ *Skills* ☑ *Insight* ☑
Grouping	*Whole Group* ☐ *2* ☐ *3* ☑ *4* ☐ *5* ☐
Time	*5-10 min* ☐ *10-15 min* ☑ *15-20 min* ☑
Anxiety	*Low* ☐ *Medium* ☑ *High* ☐
Music	*Helpful* ☐ *Not relevant* ☑
R.P.P.	*Useful for Role Play Practice* ☑

IMPROVISATION AND ROLE PLAY

III: Simulation — Life and Social Skills

21: The Knock at my Door

In this activity, group members are asked to create a scene which is as life-like as possible:

Characters: Two people unknown to each other.

Scene: A sitting room.

Action: "I was sitting quietly watching television one evening and just wondering whether to make myself a cup of tea, when there was a loud knock at my front door."

(The second character must decide who he or she is going to be — someone unknown to the owner of the house).

Discussion: After the scene has been enacted, the group may be stimulated to discuss how one might have checked who was knocking; whether there should be a chain on the door; and whether one should open the door to a stranger at night.

Key	
Focus	*Creativity* ☐ *Skills* ☑ *Insight* ☐
Grouping	*Whole Group* ☐ *2* ☑ *3* ☐ *4* ☐ *5* ☐
Time	*5-10 min* ☑ *10-15 min* ☐ *15-20 min* ☑
Anxiety	*Low* ☐ *Medium* ☑ *High* ☐
Music	*Helpful* ☐ *Not relevant* ☑
R.P.P.	*Useful for Role Play Practice* ☑

IMPROVISATION AND ROLE PLAY

III: Simulation — Life and Social Skills

22: Acting Suspiciously

As in exercise 21, the group should be urged to work towards a realistic and convincing scene.

Characters: A shop assistant; a customer; a store detective; an observer.

Scene: A department store

Action: "A shop assistant thinks that a customer is behaving suspiciously, and quietly informs the store detective. What happens?"

Discussion: It may be helpful for the whole group if small groups get together to compare endings, followed by general discussion of whether we have 'rights' in a situation such as this.

Key	
Focus	*Creativity* ☑ *Skills* ☑ *Insight* ☐
Grouping	*Whole Group* ☐ *2* ☐ *3* ☐ *4* ☑ *5* ☐
Time	*5-10 min* ☑ *10-15 min* ☑ *15-20 min* ☑
Anxiety	*Low* ☐ *Medium* ☑ *High* ☐
Music	*Helpful* ☐ *Not relevant* ☑
R.P.P.	*Useful for Role Play Practice* ☑

IMPROVISATION AND ROLE PLAY

III: Simulation — Life and Social Skills

23: Stephanie's Surprise

This exercise is introduced as in exercises 21 and 22.

Characters: Stephanie, a 20-year-old shop assistant; a foreign man; a customs official.

Scene: An airport lounge.

Action: "Stephanie is waiting to catch a plane to her dream holiday in Morocco, for which she has been saving hard. She is approached by a man. What happens?"

Discussion: Each sub-group may devise a different development and conclusion to this scene. Discussion can follow, when all groups have shared their improvisations.

Key			
Focus	*Creativity* ☑ *Skills* ☐ *Insight* ☐		
Grouping	*Whole Group* ☐ *2* ☐ *3* ☑ *4* ☐ *5* ☐		
Time	*5-10 min* ☐ *10-15 min* ☑ *15-20 min* ☑		
Anxiety	*Low* ☐ *Medium* ☑ *High* ☐		
Music	*Helpful* ☐ *Not relevant* ☑		
R.P.P.	*Useful for Role Play Practice* ☑		

IMPROVISATION AND ROLE PLAY

III: Simulation — Life and Social Skills

24: Saying No

This activity, which begins as a piece of make-believe, can be developed into more real-life scenarios.

One person takes the part of a magician who, though capable of granting many wishes, always answers 'No', whatever the request. Other group members make varied requests, some wild and fantastic, but others sensible and sincere. Some people find it very difficult to say 'no'.

Discussion of frustration/disappointment/power etc. may ensue. Members can share openly what it feels like to say 'no'.

Development/variations:
(i)   The magician may be instructed that he/she can grant *selected* wishes (eg. every third wish) but the group should not be told this.
(ii) The 'magician' should be exchanged for the real individual, to see how well he/she can continue to resist requests for money, favours etc.

Key	
Focus	*Creativity* ☐ *Skills* ☑ *Insight* ☐
Grouping	*Whole Group* ☑ *2* ☑ *3* ☑ *4* ☑ *5* ☑
Time	*5-10 min* ☐ *10-15 min* ☑ *15-20 min* ☑
Anxiety	*Low* ☐ *Medium* ☐ *High* ☑
Music	*Helpful* ☐ *Not relevant* ☑
R.P.P.	**Useful for Role Play Practice** ☑

IMPROVISATION AND ROLE PLAY

III: Simulation — Life and Social Skills

25: Persuasion

Divide the group into pairs and send each half to opposite ends of the room. One half is briefed that they work in a clothes shop and that they earn on *commission*. Whatever their partner comes into the shop to buy, alas they have not got it in stock. They should then try as hard as possible to persuade 'the customer' to buy something similar.

Meanwhile the other half is briefed that they want to buy something quite specific to wear. They must consider why they want it; the colour, the size, the design, the texture.

The leader gives the pairs a specific time for this interaction, encouraging them to reach a conclusion one way or the other. Discussion of all possible outcomes can then develop in the large group.

Key	
Focus	*Creativity* ☐ *Skills* ☑ *Insight* ☐
Grouping	*Whole Group* ☐ *2* ☑ *3* ☐ *4* ☐ *5* ☐
Time	*5-10 min* ☑ *10-15 min* ☐ *15-20 min* ☑
Anxiety	*Low* ☑ *Medium* ☐ *High* ☐
Music	*Helpful* ☐ *Not relevant* ☑
R.P.P.	*Useful for Role Play Practice* ☑

IMPROVISATION AND ROLE PLAY

III: Simulation — Life and Social Skills

26: Dissuasion

As for exercise 25, the group is divided into pairs, placed at opposite ends of the room. Brief one half that they are small shopkeepers who sell most things. When 'the customer' comes into their shop, they should contrive *not to sell them anything*, giving convincing reasons (of any sort) why they should not purchase whatever is requested.

Meanwhile the leader briefs the other partner that they need a few everyday things urgently and that the shops are due to close in ten minutes.

This role play should be developed and *resolved* in a maximum of ten minutes, after which the pairs may share their experiences with others.

Key	
Focus	*Creativity* ☐ *Skills* ☑ *Insight* ☐
Grouping	*Whole Group* ☐ *2* ☑ *3* ☐ *4* ☐ *5* ☐
Time	*5-10 min* ☑ *10-15 min* ☐ *15-20 min* ☑
Anxiety	*Low* ☐ *Medium* ☑ *High* ☐
Music	*Helpful* ☐ *Not relevant* ☑
R.P.P.	*Useful for Role Play Practice* ☑

IMPROVISATION AND ROLE PLAY

III: Simulation — Life and Social Skills

27: Presenting a Case

The leader first encourages the group to discuss why and how it is that people often complain how unfair life is, and how some people appear generally to get things whilst others do not.

Members are then divided up and given a scenario to develop.

A sum of money is potentially available and a panel has responsibility for deciding where and how it should be spent. (Allow sufficient time for rehearsal). Each group has a go at presenting their particular case to the panel who finally arrive at a verdict.

Development/variations:
(i)   Small groups may role play children and parents 'negotiating' over pocket money.
(ii)   Beggars may try to 'extract' tea money from businessmen.
(iii) Gypsies may persuade housewives to have their fortunes told.

Key	
Focus	*Creativity* ☐ *Skills* ☑ *Insight* ☐
Grouping	*Whole Group* ☐ *2* ☐ *3* ☑ *4* ☑ *5* ☑
Time	*5-10 min* ☐ *10-15 min* ☐ *15-20 min* ☑
Anxiety	*Low* ☐ *Medium* ☑ *High* ☐
Music	*Helpful* ☐ *Not relevant* ☑
R.P.P.	*Useful for Role Play Practice* ☑

III: Simulation — Life and Social Skills

28: Diplomacy

NB: For this exercise, the leader briefs the 'neighbour' to adopt a certain style or attitude eg. embarrassed/difficult/aggressive.

The situation to be role played is as follows: A letter arrives on your doorstep. You open and read it, and discover that it is *not* for you but for your next door neighbour. The letter contains some very personal information. You return the opened letter and do your best to explain what happened.

After all have tried their hand at this, the whole group discuss the most appropriate ways of dealing with the situation.

Key	
Focus	*Creativity* ☐ *Skills* ☑ *Insight* ☑
Grouping	*Whole Group* ☐ *2* ☑ *3* ☐ *4* ☐ *5* ☐
Time	*5-10 min* ☐ *10-15 min* ☑ *15-20 min* ☑
Anxiety	*Low* ☐ *Medium* ☑ *High* ☐
Music	*Helpful* ☐ *Not relevant* ☑
R.P.P.	*Useful for Role Play Practice* ☑

IMPROVISATION AND ROLE PLAY

III: Simulation — Life and Social Skills

29: Tact

For this activity, groups of three number themselves 1, 2 and 3.

The leader explains that No. 1 has invited No. 2 to a party. No. 2 then thanks No. 1 for the invitation, in front of No. 3 who has *not* been invited.

Each small group role plays and 'resolves' this scenario in a limited time. There are many different ways to handle a situation of this kind.

It may be helpful to choose the characters involved, and also their relationship to each other. Role cards may help, particularly if the group is inexperienced at role play eg. relations/friends/work colleagues.

NB: Discussion may follow this exercise.

Key	
Focus	*Creativity* ☐ *Skills* ☑ *Insight* ☐
Grouping	*Whole Group* ☐ *2* ☐ *3* ☑ *4* ☐ *5* ☐
Time	*5-10 min* ☐ *10-15 min* ☑ *15-20 min* ☑
Anxiety	*Low* ☐ *Medium* ☐ *High* ☑
Music	*Helpful* ☐ *Not relevant* ☑
R.P.P.	*Useful for Role Play Practice* ☑

IMPROVISATION AND ROLE PLAY

IV: Family Role Play

30: Suspended from School

The leader invites small groups to role play the following scene; discussion may develop afterwards in the large group.
Characters: Mother; Father; Son.
Scene: Kitchen of the family home.
Action: "The son has been suspended from school because of his hair cut. He arrives home and tells his mother. After a while, his father comes home. What transpires?"

Development/variations:
(i)   Add an elder sister who has bleached her hair.
(ii)   Instruct 'the parents' that they send the boy up to bed. Then let them role play the scene between mother and father.

Key	
Focus	*Creativity* ☐ *Skills* ☑ *Insight* ☑
Grouping	*Whole Group* ☐ *2* ☐ *3* ☑ *4* ☑ *5* ☑
Time	*5-10 min* ☐ *10-15 min* ☑ *15-20 min* ☑
Anxiety	*Low* ☐ *Medium* ☑ *High* ☐
Music	*Helpful* ☐ *Not relevant* ☑
R.P.P.	*Useful for Role Play Practice* ☑

IMPROVISATION AND ROLE PLAY

IV: Family Role Play

31: The Outsider

This exercise may involve the whole group or groups of six. Members role play the following.

Characters: A group of ex-prisoners; one new person.
Scene: A meeting room
Action: "The new person arrives for a discussion group about town planning. He has arrived in the wrong room. How do the group first discover and then explain to him that he is in the wrong group?"

Development/variations:
(i)   One ex-prisoner recognises the accidental 'intruder' as someone who used to shop-lift.
(ii)   The new person is a relative of one of the ex-prisoners and doesn't know that he/she has been in prison.

Key	
Focus	*Creativity* □ *Skills* ☑ *Insight* ☑
Grouping	*Whole Group* ☑ *2* □ *3* □ *4* □ *5* ☑
Time	*5-10 min* □ *10-15 min* ☑ *15-20 min* ☑
Anxiety	*Low* □ *Medium* ☑ *High* □
Music	*Helpful* □ *Not relevant* ☑
R.P.P.	*Useful for Role Play Practice* ☑

IMPROVISATION AND ROLE PLAY

IV: Family Role Play

32: Something Awful Happened

This is a make-believe role play which the leader can make as realistic or as fantastic as seems appropriate to the group's needs.

Characters: Families, with or without children.
Scene: The family sitting room.
Action: "One family member arrives home and says that something awful happened . . ."

NB: There should be some initial discussion of who will take which role, and what the characters in the family are like.

After the exercise discussion may develop on 'awful' things which have really happened in members' own families.

Key	
Focus	*Creativity* ☐ *Skills* ☑ *Insight* ☑
Grouping	*Whole Group* ☐ *2* ☑ *3* ☐ *4* ☑ *5* ☐
Time	*5-10 min* ☐ *10-15 min* ☑ *15-20 min* ☑
Anxiety	*Low* ☐ *Medium* ☐ *High* ☑
Music	*Helpful* ☐ *Not relevant* ☑
R.P.P.	*Useful for Role Play Practice* ☑

IMPROVISATION AND ROLE PLAY

IV: Family Role Play

33: Family Secrets

The leader invites members to divide into small groups, to 'create' a family, and to decide what secret that family choose to keep hidden.

Characters: A family (members to be decided).
Scene: Family living room.
Action: The family have an unhappy or guilty secret (eg. one member in prison; one pregnant; one at odds with the rest). A visitor arrives, and the family try to keep the secret to themselves.

Development/variations:

The visitor is a police officer who has arrived with the purpose of asking questions about a crime.

NB: It is highly likely that the group will want to discuss many aspects of the above situations, if sufficient time is made available.

Key	
Focus	*Creativity* ☑ *Skills* ☐ *Insight* ☑
Grouping	*Whole Group* ☐ *2* ☐ *3* ☑ *4* ☑ *5* ☑
Time	*5-10 min* ☑ *10-15 min* ☑ *15-20 min* ☑
Anxiety	*Low* ☐ *Medium* ☐ *High* ☑
Music	*Helpful* ☐ *Not relevant* ☑
R.P.P.	*Useful for Role Play Practice* ☑

IMPROVISATION
AND ROLE PLAY

IV: Family Role Play

34: Not Granny Again

Members create a family group, or groups, which includes a granny or grandpa. They decide precisely what the family is like, where they live etc.

Characters: A family of three generations; a visitor.

Scene: The family living room.

Action: Granny is very 'difficult'. A visitor calls and the family *endeavour* to behave as if everything is fine! What does the visitor do? What are the problems encountered by the family?

NB: This activity is certain to stimulate discussion especially if any members have direct experience of this type of difficulty.

Key	
Focus	*Creativity* ☐ *Skills* ☑ *Insight* ☑
Grouping	*Whole Group* ☐ *2* ☐ *3* ☐ *4* ☑ *5* ☑
Time	*5-10 min* ☐ *10-15 min* ☑ *15-20 min* ☑
Anxiety	*Low* ☐ *Medium* ☐ *High* ☑
Music	*Helpful* ☐ *Not relevant* ☑
R.P.P.	*Useful for Role Play Practice* ☑

IMPROVISATION AND ROLE PLAY

IV: Family Role Play

35: Family Decisions

The leader can introduce this activity by stimulating group discussion on what happens when families have decisions to make. Are people 'told' what to do? Who makes decisions? Are they usually negotiated?

The group is then divided into 'family groups', and members can discuss who will take each role within the family. The families are then presented with a decision to make, eg. where shall we go on holiday? How should we spend £100? Should we move?

Development/variations:
(i)   Members receive family role cards which describe each role in some detail.
(ii) The whole group may be invited to decide what types of decision would be difficult for the different role-played families to make.

Key	
Focus	*Creativity* ☑ *Skills* ☑ *Insight* ☑
Grouping	*Whole Group* ☐ *2* ☐ *3* ☐ *4* ☑ *5* ☑
Time	*5-10 min* ☐ *10-15 min* ☑ *15-20 min* ☑
Anxiety	*Low* ☐ *Medium* ☑ *High* ☐
Music	*Helpful* ☐ *Not relevant* ☑
R.P.P.	*Useful for Role Play Practice* ☑

VISUAL DYNAMICS

I: Sculpting

1: Free Sculpt: Here and Now Feelings

It may be necessary to explain first to the group what a 'sculpt' is: it is a means of representing how people are feeling, yet presented in a static, visual way — rather like a still photograph.

The leader invites members to place themselves in the room to represent "how *you* are feeling now, in relation to everyone else"

This activity may be introduced by some related role play. Clusters, sub-groups, pairings — and some outsiders — emerge.

Then participants place themselves where they would *like* to be in relation to everyone else. This may be followed up by some discussion of what it entails to move from one position to the other.

Development/variations:

Let the sculpt be 'mobile' with movements and sounds which members feel appropriate to their position in the group.

Key	
Focus	*Creativity* ☐ *Skills* ☐ *Insight* ☑
Grouping	*Whole Group* ☑ *2* ☐ *3* ☐ *4* ☐ *5* ☐
Time	*5-10 min* ☐ *10-15 min* ☑ *15-20 min* ☑
Anxiety	*Low* ☑ *Medium* ☑ *High* ☐
Music	*Helpful* ☐ *Not relevant* ☑
R.P.P.	*Useful for Role Play Practice* ☐

I: Sculpting

2: Free Sculpt: Thematic

The leader should first check that the group members understand what is meant by a 'sculpt'.

Members are then asked to place themselves in the room to represent their perception of a relevant theme, eg. "This institution" (members may choose to respond by portraying aspects of authority or by identifying a hierarchy.)

NB: If individuals are inclined to produce caricatures of absent members of staff, they should be encouraged to represent *present* dynamics. The material which emerges may be used either to help the group itself, or as a way of bringing about change in the institution.

Key	
Focus	*Creativity* ☐ *Skills* ☐ *Insight* ☑
Grouping	*Whole Group* ☑ *2* ☐ *3* ☐ *4* ☐ *5* ☐
Time	*5-10 min* ☐ *10-15 min* ☑ *15-20 min* ☑
Anxiety	*Low* ☑ *Medium* ☑ *High* ☐
Music	*Helpful* ☐ *Not relevant* ☑
R.P.P.	*Useful for Role Play Practice* ☐

I: Sculpting

3: Free Sculpt: Metaphor

The leader chooses a metaphor for people to use as a sculpt, and describes it well, eg. "Our group room is a swimming pool, which occupies most of the floor space. There are deep and shallow ends, a springboard, high diving boards, and an area to sit in with tables and chairs and sun umbrellas. Position yourselves in this scene to represent how you see yourselves in relation to the whole group."

NB: It is advisable to 'stay with' the metaphor, *not* attempting to interpret what is conveyed by members by putting it into everyday language. Some surprises may need to be checked out, and members may like to work with changes they would wish to make, eg. someone with only a toe in the water at the shallow end may be keen to try swimming across the centre.

Key	
Focus	*Creativity* ☐ *Skills* ☐ *Insight* ☑
Grouping	*Whole Group* ☑ *2* ☐ *3* ☐ *4* ☐ *5* ☐
Time	*5-10 min* ☐ *10-15 min* ☑ *15-20 min* ☑
Anxiety	*Low* ☐ *Medium* ☑ *High* ☑
Music	*Helpful* ☐ *Not relevant* ☑
R.P.P.	*Useful for Role Play Practice* ☐

VISUAL DYNAMICS

I: Sculpting

4: Free Sculpt: Diagonal

The leader selects two polarities which have become apparent in the group, eg. trust/mistrust:

Members are then asked to place themselves along a diagonal that represents the two extremes, eg

Trust
(ie. I trust people
very easily)

Mistrust
(ie. I don't trust
people at all)

There may emerge some surprises which should be checked out. Group members may then be asked to place themselves along the diagonal where they would *like* to be, and then to discuss the discrepancies and work with the change this would entail, perhaps through role play.

Key	
Focus	*Creativity* ☐ *Skills* ☐ *Insight* ☑
Grouping	*Whole Group* ☑ *2* ☐ *3* ☐ *4* ☐ *5* ☐
Time	*5-10 min* ☐ *10-15 min* ☑ *15-20 min* ☑
Anxiety	*Low* ☐ *Medium* ☑ *High* ☐
Music	*Helpful* ☐ *Not relevant* ☑
R.P.P.	*Useful for Role Play Practice* ☐

VISUAL DYNAMICS

I: Sculpting

5: Directed Sculpts: Here and Now Feelings

One member of the group is invited to arrange everyone else to represent their perception of the group. Suggest that he or she works quickly and intuitively, rather than thinking it out. That same member should then be asked to 'double' the spaces and the people — that is to say to *speak on behalf* of others, eg. "I'm standing here because . . ." or "In this space I feel cold and lonely."

NB: It is quite usual for other members of the same group to have very different views of the group, in which case each should be encouraged to sculpt his or her perception, rather than to talk about it. Contrasting views may later be compared and discussed, and differences may be used constructively through role play.

Key	
Focus	*Creativity* ☐ *Skills* ☐ *Insight* ☑
Grouping	*Whole Group* ☑ *2* ☐ *3* ☐ *4* ☐ *5* ☐
Time	*5-10 min* ☐ *10-15 min* ☐ *15-20 min* ☑
Anxiety	*Low* ☐ *Medium* ☑ *High* ☐
Music	*Helpful* ☐ *Not relevant* ☑
R.P.P.	*Useful for Role Play Practice* ☐

VISUAL DYNAMICS

I: Sculpting

6: Directed Sculpts: Thematic

Here, the leader invites a member of the group to place others on a diagonal between polarities, eg.

Individuals should then be allowed to respond to where they have been placed. This sculpt could then develop into work around such statements as:

"Other people see me as . . . whereas inside I always feel . . ."

"My father always said I was . . ., but I always felt . . ."

Key	
Focus	*Creativity* ☐ *Skills* ☐ *Insight* ☑
Grouping	*Whole Group* ☑ *2* ☐ *3* ☐ *4* ☐ *5* ☐
Time	*5-10 min* ☐ *10-15 min* ☐ *15-20 min* ☑
Anxiety	*Low* ☐ *Medium* ☑ *High* ☐
Music	*Helpful* ☐ *Not relevant* ☑
R.P.P.	*Useful for Role Play Practice* ☐

VISUAL DYNAMICS

I: Sculpting

7: Directed Sculpts: Metaphor

It may be necessary first to discuss with the group how we use metaphors to talk about ourselves and our world, eg. "my heart is full to bursting; my life is a burden; you have been a light on the path."

The leader then asks one person to sculpt the group around a metaphor, eg. "If this group was a farm, who would everybody be?".

NB: Members should always be encouraged to work intuitively and to take leaps of imagination, eg. in the example above, members need not represent solely people or animals, but crops, machinery or buildings. If other group members volunteer some alternative metaphors, such as "This group is more like a circus", then follow these ideas through.

Key	
Focus	*Creativity* ☑ *Skills* ☑ *Insight* ☑
Grouping	*Whole Group* ☑ *2* ☐ *3* ☐ *4* ☐ *5* ☐
Time	*5-10 min* ☐ *10-15 min* ☑ *15-20 min* ☑
Anxiety	*Low* ☐ *Medium* ☐ *High* ☑
Music	*Helpful* ☐ *Not relevant* ☑
R.P.P.	*Useful for Role Play Practice* ☐

VISUAL DYNAMICS

I: Sculpting

8: Chair Sculpts: Important People

The leader explains that chairs are to be used to represent people who are, or have been, important influences in the lives of members of the group.

A maximum of 4 chairs should be used. Ensure that members identify positive as well as negative influences.

In turn, individuals should sit in each chair they have assigned a role or position to and 'introduce them' by doubling. That is to say, they should speak on behalf of the person represented, saying how that person has influenced the individual who devised the sculpt.

When all the chairs have 'spoken', the individual should respond by saying something to each of those 'important people'.

Key	
Focus	*Creativity* ☐ *Skills* ☐ *Insight* ☑
Grouping	*Whole Group* ☑ *2* ☐ *3* ☐ *4* ☐ *5* ☐
Time	*5-10 min* ☐ *10-15 min* ☐ *15-20 min* ☑
Anxiety	*Low* ☐ *Medium* ☑ *High* ☐
Music	*Helpful* ☐ *Not relevant* ☑
R.P.P.	*Useful for Role Play Practice* ☐

I: Sculpting

9: Chair Sculpts: Then and Now

Three chairs are placed in a line thus:

The leader then explains that Chair 1 represents one individual in the group — as he/she was 5 years ago; Chair 2 represents now; and Chair 3 represents 5 years into the future.
That person should then sit in each chair in turn and talk about himself/herself at each stage.
NB: 5 years may be too long a time scale for some groups to conceptualize, or to make predictions about. Therefore, the leader should be prepared to adjust the scale to an appropriate time span.

Development/variations:
(i) The three chairs may represent "you as a child; you now; and you in old age".

Key	
Focus	*Creativity* ☐ *Skills* ☐ *Insight* ☑
Grouping	*Whole Group* ☑ *2* ☐ *3* ☐ *4* ☐ *5* ☐
Time	*5-10 min* ☐ *10-15 min* ☐ *15-20 min* ☑
Anxiety	*Low* ☐ *Medium* ☑ *High* ☑
Music	*Helpful* ☐ *Not relevant* ☑
R.P.P.	*Useful for Role Play Practice* ☐

VISUAL DYNAMICS

II: Spectograms

10: Using Free Objects

For this activity, many assorted small objects are used to create a representation of "My life now".

The leader sets a limit of 5 minutes, and explains that anything at all — jewellery, watches, coins, keys, pens, etc — may be used to represent people, places, objects, feelings etc.

Later, two or three members can share their spectograms and answer questions on them. However, partners should *not* attempt to interpret what is offered in reply. Ensure that all members of the group are given enough time to create a spectogram.

Encourage individuals to readjust the spectogram to represent how they would like their life to look. Objects may be removed, moved, augmented etc. These changes should then be shared with partners and discussed, emphasizing how changes can be made *in small steps*.

Make sure objects are 'de-roled' before the session is finished (see no. 11).

Key	
Focus	*Creativity* ☐ *Skills* ☐ *Insight* ☑
Grouping	*Whole Group* ☑ *2* ☑ *3* ☐ *4* ☐ *5* ☐
Time	*5-10 min* ☐ *10-15 min* ☐ *15-20 min* ☑
Anxiety	*Low* ☐ *Medium* ☑ *High* ☑
Music	*Helpful* ☐ *Not relevant* ☑
R.P.P.	*Useful for Role Play Practice* ☐

VISUAL DYNAMICS

II: Spectograms

11: Using Given Objects

This activity is similar to No. 10, except that the objects are already provided. Beads, buttons, marbles, rosettes, buckles, suspenders etc. are all supplied in a large box or tin.

   Members are each given a turn to create a representation of their life; or their family; or their role at work etc. A record of these may be made for future use, say when trying the exercise again in 3 months and making comparisons.
NB: As in No. 10, it is extremely important to de-role the objects before putting them back in the box, eg. "This fat marble was my boss but now it is a marble again".

Development/variations:
(i)   Consider what aspects of people's spectograms are inevitable.
(ii) Consider which aspects they have autonomy over.
(iii) Consider possible changes and discuss them.

Key	
Focus	*Creativity* ☐ *Skills* ☐ *Insight* ☑
Grouping	*Whole Group* ☑ *2* ☑ *3* ☐ *4* ☐ *5* ☐
Time	*5-10 min* ☐ *10-15 min* ☐ *15-20 min* ☑
Anxiety	*Low* ☐ *Medium* ☑ *High* ☑
Music	*Helpful* ☐ *Not relevant* ☑
R.P.P.	*Useful for Role Play Practice* ☐

VISUAL DYNAMICS

II: Spectograms

12: Russian Nesting Dolls

The leader warms up the group to this exercise by letting them examine the Russian dolls and discuss them. There is usually a lot of curiosity about the very small ones in the middle.

Members are then encouraged to use the dolls to make statements about people in their lives, eg. "These are the people bigger than me and these are the people smaller than me."

Development/variations:
(i)   Members choose dolls to represent those they *perceive* as being more or less significant/important/capable/strong than themselves.
(ii) Ask them to tell a story, using the Russian nesting dolls as characters. Usually, these stories tend to be somewhat autobiographical, at least in parts.

Key	
Focus	*Creativity* ☐ *Skills* ☑ *Insight* ☑
Grouping	*Whole Group* ☑ *2* ☑ *3* ☐ *4* ☐ *5* ☐
Time	*5-10 min* ☐ *10-15 min* ☑ *15-20 min* ☑
Anxiety	*Low* ☐ *Medium* ☑ *High* ☑
Music	*Helpful* ☐ *Not relevant* ☑
R.P.P.	*Useful for Role Play Practice* ☐

II: Spectograms

13: Animals (See Appendix for examples)

For this activity, a large supply of toy farm or wild animals is needed. Group members are asked to represent a scene or a stage in their lives by using the animals, eg. "My feelings now".

Different animals represent contrasting aspects of themselves. People can get 'in touch' with denied aspects of themselves or illustrate a quality they would like to have.

NB: Creating the 'pictures', sharing and reflecting, is helpful to many. Others may benefit from further role play based upon this material.

Key	
Focus	*Creativity* ☐ *Skills* ☐ *Insight* ☑
Grouping	*Whole Group* ☑ *2* ☑ *3* ☐ *4* ☐ *5* ☐
Time	*5-10 min* ☐ *10-15 min* ☑ *15-20 min* ☑
Anxiety	*Low* ☐ *Medium* ☑ *High* ☑
Music	*Helpful* ☐ *Not relevant* ☑
R.P.P.	*Useful for Role Play Practice* ☐

II: Spectograms

14: Miniatures (see appendix for examples)

The leader supplies a range of small figures, pottery ornaments, dolls house people etc. Members can then play with the people and look at them well before choosing which to use in creating a spectogram.

The group may *either* be given the title of a scene to create, eg. leaving home; *or* they may be asked to represent an important scene from their own lives.

Members can share what they have created, with a partner, and work on it if appropriate, eg. "My mother didn't want me to leave home."

Key	
Focus	*Creativity* ☐ *Skills* ☐ *Insight* ☑
Grouping	*Whole Group* ☑ *2* ☑ *3* ☐ *4* ☐ *5* ☐
Time	*5-10 min* ☐ *10-15 min* ☑ *15-20 min* ☑
Anxiety	*Low* ☐ *Medium* ☑ *High* ☑
Music	*Helpful* ☐ *Not relevant* ☑
R.P.P.	*Useful for Role Play Practice* ☐

VISUAL DYNAMICS

III: Pictograms

15: Mapping

For this exercise, felt tip pens, crayons and large sheets of paper are needed. Members are asked to close their eyes and to imagine the sort of environment they would like to live in. What sort of things are nearby? — mountains, sea, houses, discos?

Then, they are asked to draw a map of the place they have imagined, putting in signs to indicate where other resources and features are, eg City ——➤ 7 miles.

Individuals could then join in pairs or small groups, to share the different maps and 'visions'.

Development/variations:
(i)   Get all group members to combine their maps to form one large imaginary place.
(ii) Divide members into small groups according to similar elements in their individual maps; and encourage them to discuss their ideal community.

Key	
Focus	*Creativity* ☐ *Skills* ☑ *Insight* ☑
Grouping	*Whole Group* ☑ *2* ☐ *3* ☑ *4* ☑ *5* ☑
Time	*5-10 min* ☐ *10-15 min* ☑ *15-20 min* ☑
Anxiety	*Low* ☐ *Medium* ☑ *High* ☐
Music	*Helpful* ☐ *Not relevant* ☑
R.P.P.	*Useful for Role Play Practice* ☐

VISUAL DYNAMICS

III: Pictograms

16: Pathways

For this activity, felt tip pens, crayons and large sheets of paper are required. Members are first asked to close their eyes and imagine their lives as pathways. How far back can they see along the path? What shape does it have? Are there some curves, some straight sections and some *very* twisty bits? Is the path rough in parts?

When members have opened their eyes they should *draw* the pathway from 'the beginning' to the present, adding in signs/symbols/words for significnt events. These pictograms can then be shared with partners and members can state where they would like the path to go in the future.

Development/variations:
(i)   The pathway may specifically depict a journey through illness and health.
(ii) The whole group may co-operate in drawing a path showing the life of the group since it first started.

Key	
Focus	*Creativity* ☐ *Skills* ☑ *Insight* ☑
Grouping	*Whole Group* ☑ *2* ☐ *3* ☐ *4* ☐ *5* ☐
Time	*5-10 min* ☐ *10-15 min* ☑ *15-20 min* ☑
Anxiety	*Low* ☑ *Medium* ☑ *High* ☐
Music	*Helpful* ☐ *Not relevant* ☑
R.P.P.	*Useful for Role Play Practice* ☐

III: Pictograms

17: Houses

For this exercise, glue, scissors, staples, shoe boxes, string, sugar paper, plasticine, felt tip pens and paints are necessary.

Non-institutionalized groups can be asked to supply their own shoe boxes.

Members close their eyes, relax, and imagine the word 'house'. What sort of house comes to mind? *Their* house; an imaginary house; their childhood home; a dream house?

Considering many different images, they should decide what house they are going to create for themselves.

In *20 minutes*, each person creates a house to his/her own design.

The activity, and the end product, will naturally vary according to the age and capabilities of group members. Ask people to tell the story of their house. What has it seen since it was built? Who lives there now?

Key	
Focus	*Creativity* ☐ *Skills* ☐ *Insight* ☑
Grouping	*Whole Group* ☑ *2* ☐ *3* ☐ *4* ☐ *5* ☐
Time	*5-10 min* ☐ *10-15 min* ☑ *15-20 min* ☑
Anxiety	*Low* ☐ *Medium* ☑ *High* ☐
Music	*Helpful* ☐ *Not relevant* ☑
R.P.P.	*Useful for Role Play Practice* ☐

VISUAL DYNAMICS

III: Pictograms

18: Miniature Houses

For this exercise, trays or model boards and plasticine are required. It is best to work this group activity around a large table.

Instruct the group to "imagine your ideal home — be it cottage or castle — and make it in miniature with the plasticine in *no more than 15 minutes*.

Working in miniature is often less frightening than work on a large scale, and groups frequently take great delight in creating the tiny buildings. When they are completed, members can 'share' their ideal houses by talking about them. A community may then be created, by grouping all the buildings together according to who lives near who or what, eg. a town, open country, a best friend, the shopping centre.

Key	
Focus	*Creativity* ☐ *Skills* ☑ *Insight* ☑
Grouping	*Whole Group* ☑ *2* ☐ *3* ☐ *4* ☐ *5* ☐
Time	*5-10 min* ☐ *10-15 min* ☑ *15-20 min* ☑
Anxiety	*Low* ☑ *Medium* ☑ *High* ☐
Music	*Helpful* ☐ *Not relevant* ☑
R.P.P.	*Useful for Role Play Practice* ☐

VISUAL DYNAMICS

III: Pictograms

19: Group Relations

A *large* piece of paper is necessary for this exercise — place it on a big table or preferably on the floor. A good supply of felt tip pens, paints and toy animals is also required.

The leader puts out all the animals and asks the group to make a choice of *one only*, having scanned them all very quickly. Each individual should place an animal on the paper and create an environment for it. Members tend to vary in their responses: some spread over a wide space while others have a clearly defined patch which they have 'claimed' for their animal.

When each person has finished, the whole group should consider the overall layout, perhaps linking some areas by roads etc.

Members may wish to devise a story about the group picture, or describe an incident in the life of one animal.

Key	
Focus	*Creativity* ☐ *Skills* ☑ *Insight* ☑
Grouping	*Whole Group* ☑ *2* ☐ *3* ☐ *4* ☐ *5* ☐
Time	*5-10 min* ☐ *10-15 min* ☑ *15-20 min* ☑
Anxiety	*Low* ☑ *Medium* ☑ *High* ☐
Music	*Helpful* ☐ *Not relevant* ☑
R.P.P.	*Useful for Role Play Practice* ☐

III: Pictograms

20: Collage

For this activity, felt tip pens or wax crayons, sugar paper, glue, scissors and a wide variety of old magazines are required.

First, there should be general discussion about images and pictures. For example, what advertisements and pictures do most people notice? Which are silly; strong; effective?

Members should then be invited to make up their own pictures, describing "My Life Now". They may choose whatever size of sugar paper they wish, and include anything that they want in the picture. A time limit should be given, and members may wish to 'share' their collages when they are completed. Constructive questions may be put by other group members, and the exercise may lead to some role play.

Key	
Focus	*Creativity* ☐ *Skills* ☐ *Insight* ☑
Grouping	*Whole Group* ☑ *2* ☐ *3* ☐ *4* ☐ *5* ☐
Time	*5-10 min* ☐ *10-15 min* ☑ *15-20 min* ☑
Anxiety	*Low* ☑ *Medium* ☑ *High* ☐
Music	*Helpful* ☐ *Not relevant* ☑
R.P.P.	*Useful for Role Play Practice* ☐

VISUAL DYNAMICS

IV: Family Trees

21: My Life in Context

For this exercise, large sheets of paper and felt tip pens are required.

Members are asked to represent three generations of their families in a family tree, if they can, using a chosen colour to represent themselves.

KEY: △ — men   eg.
       ○ — women
       = — married
       ≠ — separated
           or divorced

Particular colours may be chosen to represent significant people in their lives. Black may be used to show that someone has died.

These family trees can be 'shared' with other group members.

Key	
Focus	*Creativity* ☐ *Skills* ☐ *Insight* ☑
Grouping	*Whole Group* ☑ *2* ☐ *3* ☑ *4* ☑ *5* ☑
Time	*5-10 min* ☐ *10-15 min* ☑ *15-20 min* ☑
Anxiety	*Low* ☐ *Medium* ☑ *High* ☑
Music	*Helpful* ☐ *Not relevant* ☑
R.P.P.	*Useful for Role Play Practice* ☐

VISUAL DYNAMICS

IV: Family Trees

22: People Like Me/People Not Like Me

Again, large sheets of paper and felt pens are required. Each individual can create a family tree, as in exercise 21, and then add labels to describe each person the member can actually remember, eg. lovable rogue; pretty and dull; quiet but friendly; bad tempered.

Members should consider carefully which words they would choose to describe themselves, and which words *others* might use to describe them.

These family trees and adjectives may then be shared, and possibly role played, with a partner or in a small group.

Key	
Focus	*Creativity* ☐ *Skills* ☑ *Insight* ☑
Grouping	*Whole Group* ☑ *2* ☐ *3* ☑ *4* ☑ *5* ☐
Time	*5-10 min* ☐ *10-15 min* ☑ *15-20 min* ☑
Anxiety	*Low* ☐ *Medium* ☑ *High* ☐
Music	*Helpful* ☐ *Not relevant* ☑
R.P.P.	*Useful for Role Play Practice* ☐

VISUAL DYNAMICS

IV: Family Trees

23: Family History

In this activity, miniature people, small toys and animals are used to create a three-dimensional family tree, putting in as many people as members can recall.

The story of the family tree can be shared with a partner when it is complete, and each individual is encouraged to describe who they feel they are like or unlike in the picture they have given.

NB: Some clients would be too vulnerable to benefit from such an exercise. The leader should be careful that this activity is really appropriate for a particular group. 'Life at a glance' exercises may distress some people.

Key	
Focus	*Creativity* □ *Skills* □ *Insight* ☑
Grouping	*Whole Group* ☑ *2* ☑ *3* □ *4* □ *5* □
Time	*5-10 min* □ *10-15 min* ☑ *15-20 min* ☑
Anxiety	*Low* □ *Medium* ☑ *High* □
Music	*Helpful* □ *Not relevant* ☑
R.P.P.	*Useful for Role Play Practice* □

VISUAL DYNAMICS

V: Masks

24: My Feelings

For this exercise, felt pens, crayons, card templates (ready prepared) and paper are required. Using a cut-out template, members draw for themselves:
- (i)   an angry mask
- (ii) a happy mask

They should then 'share' their different appearances with the group, holding a mask in front of the face and speaking in an appropriate tone, eg. "When I am angry . . ."

Development/variations:

(i)   Use role play to talk with angry masks to someone else's happy or angry mask.

(ii) Whilst wearing angry masks, members talk about who in their lives make them feel angry.

Key	
Focus	*Creativity* ☐ *Skills* ☐ *Insight* ☑
Grouping	*Whole Group* ☑ *2* ☑ *3* ☐ *4* ☐ *5* ☐
Time	*5-10 min* ☐ *10-15 min* ☑ *15-20 min* ☑
Anxiety	*Low* ☐ *Medium* ☑ *High* ☑
Music	*Helpful* ☐ *Not relevant* ☑
R.P.P.	*Useful for Role Play Practice* ☑

VISUAL DYNAMICS

V: Masks

25: Public and Private

Card templates, felt pens, crayons and paper are again required.

Members are asked to close their eyes and picture their 'public' face, and then to draw a mask to represent the face the world sees — perhaps the face each individual sees in the mirror.

Secondly, members close their eyes and conjure up a picture of a more private face that perhaps people do not see so often. This face, too, is drawn on a mask.

These masks are, in turn, held up in front of the face while a member makes a statement.

Development/variations:

Let partners introduce each other to the whole group, using their partners' masks.

Key	
Focus	*Creativity* □ *Skills* □ *Insight* ☑
Grouping	*Whole Group* ☑ *2* ☑ *3* □ *4* □ *5* □
Time	*5-10 min* □ *10-15 min* □ *15-20 min* ☑
Anxiety	*Low* □ *Medium* ☑ *High* ☑
Music	*Helpful* □ *Not relevant* ☑
R.P.P.	*Useful for Role Play Practice* ☑

VISUAL DYNAMICS

V: Masks

26: Different Feelings

Again, card templates, felt pens, crayons and paper are required.

Group members are given a template and paper and asked to draw more than one mask to represent different feelings they have experienced during the day.

These feelings should be shared by using the masks, with other group members. Feelings which arise frequently may be discussed.

Development/variations:
(i)   Create past, present and future feelings on masks.
(ii) Feelings which are inside and difficult to express may be represented on masks.
(iii) Members may like to draw a 'feeling' face which they would like to experience in reality more often.

Key	
Focus	*Creativity* ☐ *Skills* ☐ *Insight* ☑
Grouping	*Whole Group* ☑ *2* ☑ *3* ☐ *4* ☐ *5* ☐
Time	*5-10 min* ☐ *10-15 min* ☑ *15-20 min* ☑
Anxiety	*Low* ☐ *Medium* ☑ *High* ☑
Music	*Helpful* ☐ *Not relevant* ☑
R.P.P.	*Useful for Role Play Practice* ☑

VISUAL DYNAMICS

V: Masks

27: Before and After

This exercise requires felt pens, crayons, paper and cardboard templates.

At the very beginning of a session, members are asked to draw a mask representing how they feel. A second mask is drawn towards the end of the session, and the 'before and after' faces can be compared and discussed. This is a useful exercise for illustrating how people can move, change, experience things differently etc.

The faces can be kept in a folder for future use. The group may be asked to do the same thing after, perhaps, a six week interval; then both sets of masks can be compared.

Key	
Focus	*Creativity* ☐ *Skills* ☑ *Insight* ☑
Grouping	*Whole Group* ☑ *2* ☐ *3* ☐ *4* ☐ *5* ☐
Time	*5-10 min* ☑ *10-15 min* ☑ *15-20 min* ☑
Anxiety	*Low* ☑ *Medium* ☑ *High* ☑
Music	*Helpful* ☐ *Not relevant* ☑
R.P.P.	*Useful for Role Play Practice* ☐

V: Masks

28: Diary

Felt tip pens, crayons, templates and paper are required for
these masks. This exercise can also be used as a closure
activity.

Members draw round the template a number of times and
staple several together to form a book (eg. ten masks for a
ten-week group).

At the end of each group, a mask can be coloured in as a way
of recording feelings instead of writing or talking about them.

During the last session, the series of masks may be studied,
and a 'journey through the masks' can be shared with other
group members.

NB: The book's cover should also be coloured and given a title.

Key	
Focus	*Creativity* ☐ *Skills* ☐ *Insight* ☑
Grouping	*Whole Group* ☑ *2* ☐ *3* ☐ *4* ☐ *5* ☐
Time	*5-10 min* ☐ *10-15 min* ☑ *15-20 min* ☑
Anxiety	*Low* ☐ *Medium* ☑ *High* ☑
Music	*Helpful* ☐ *Not relevant* ☑
R.P.P.	*Useful for Role Play Practice* ☐

VISUAL DYNAMICS

V: Masks

29: Dreams

Felt tips, crayons, templates and paper are required for these masks.

Members create faces of important characters in a dream, or a favourite myth or story. The masks can be used to explore the dream and to become the different characters. Other group members can 'become' the people in the dream too.

Development/variations:
(i) A story may be made up and illustrated with masks. The story can be told to the group, using only the masks or involving some group members as characters.
(ii) The story may be devised by the whole group in co-operation.

Key	
Focus	*Creativity* ☐ *Skills* ☐ *Insight* ☑
Grouping	*Whole Group* ☑ *2* ☐ *3* ☐ *4* ☐ *5* ☐
Time	*5-10 min* ☐ *10-15 min* ☐ *15-20 min* ☑
Anxiety	*Low* ☐ *Medium* ☑ *High* ☑
Music	*Helpful* ☐ *Not relevant* ☑
R.P.P.	*Useful for Role Play Practice* ☐

VISUAL DYNAMICS

V: Masks

30: Different Roles

Using templates or plasticene, or a combination of both, the group create three different masks each, to represent themselves at different life stages, eg. when they were very young, when they reach old age, when they are middle aged.

This is a useful exercise before developing role play, providing one means of projecting into different roles.

If group members are not anxious about this activity, they may feel happy to talk about themselves at the different life stages, from behind the appropriate masks. However, if they lack confidence or feel anxious, it may be less stressful to make plasticene masks on a small scale and talk about them.

Key	
Focus	*Creativity* ☐ *Skills* ☐ *Insight* ☑
Grouping	*Whole Group* ☑ *2* ☐ *3* ☐ *4* ☐ *5* ☐
Time	*5-10 min* ☐ *10-15 min* ☑ *15-20 min* ☑
Anxiety	*Low* ☐ *Medium* ☑ *High* ☑
Music	*Helpful* ☐ *Not relevant* ☑
R.P.P.	*Useful for Role Play Practice* ☑

Closure
Phase

CLOSURES

I: De-roling

1: Role Change

After being involved in a role play exercise, it is essential that members be given an opportunity to *de-role*. This can be achieved in various ways, one of which is to close their eyes and picture in the mind's eye the character they have just played. That character should be visualised walking away down the road, turning a corner and waving before being lost to sight.

This done, members can open their eyes and share with each other what it felt like to play the role in question. If any of that role is 'still with them', they should talk it through with the group and decide what aspects of that character or situation to set down or 'give up', and what to absorb.

Key	
Focus	*Creativity* ☑ *Skills* ☐ *Insight* ☑
Grouping	*Whole Group* ☑ *2* ☐ *3* ☐ *4* ☐ *5* ☐
Time	*5-10 min* ☐ *10-15 min* ☑ *15-20 min* ☐
Anxiety	*Low* ☑ *Medium* ☑ *High* ☐
Music	*Helpful* ☐ *Not relevant* ☑
R.P.P.	*Useful for Role Play Practice* ☑

CLOSURES

I: De-roling

2: Family Roles

If the group have been role playing someone's family, the leader should indicate to that member how he or she can de-role the rest of the participants by "doubling" (namely by talking on their behalf), eg. "I am no longer Mary's mother who . . ., but I am Penny Jones who . . ."

Following the above statement, Penny Jones should repeat what has just been said about her, and then share with other members how it felt to play the role of Mary's mother.

Development/variations:

Participants in the role play can later discuss what they identified with, and what did *not* feel like them.

Key	
Focus	*Creativity* ☐ *Skills* ☐ *Insight* ☑
Grouping	*Whole Group* ☑ *2* ☐ *3* ☐ *4* ☐ *5* ☐
Time	*5-10 min* ☑ *10-15 min* ☐ *15-20 min* ☐
Anxiety	*Low* ☐ *Medium* ☑ *High* ☑
Music	*Helpful* ☐ *Not relevant* ☑
R.P.P.	*Useful for Role Play Practice* ☐

CLOSURES

I: De-roling

3: Non-verbal: Movement

At the end of a role play, the leader asks the group to close their eyes and picture the person they have just portrayed. They should visualise how he/she moved, and begin to make those movements, gestures or mannerisms in an exaggerated way. Then, very slowly, limb by limb, they should begin to revert to their *own* way of moving, at first exaggerated and later becoming perfectly normal again.

After walking around the room 'as themselves' for a while, members gradually come to a standstill.

Key	
Focus	*Creativity* ☑ *Skills* ☐ *Insight* ☑
Grouping	*Whole Group* ☑ *2* ☐ *3* ☐ *4* ☐ *5* ☐
Time	*5-10 min* ☐ *10-15 min* ☑ *15-20 min* ☐
Anxiety	*Low* ☑ *Medium* ☐ *High* ☐
Music	*Helpful* ☑ *Not relevant* ☐
R.P.P.	*Useful for Role Play Practice* ☐

CLOSURES

I: De-roling

4: Non-verbal: Objects

The leader explains to group members how to place a chair in front of them and to 'place' the role they have just played on to that chair. In their imaginations, they see the characters sitting on those chairs. Can they picture what they are wearing? What colours? What style? Several minutes should be spent visualizing those people and, as this is taking place, members should feel themselves becoming their real selves again.

Each person should walk away from the chair as *him or herself*.

Key	
Focus	*Creativity* ☐ *Skills* ☑ *Insight* ☑
Grouping	*Whole Group* ☑ *2* ☐ *3* ☐ *4* ☐ *5* ☐
Time	*5-10 min* ☑ *10-15 min* ☐ *15-20 min* ☐
Anxiety	*Low* ☑ *Medium* ☑ *High* ☐
Music	*Helpful* ☐ *Not relevant* ☑
R.P.P.	*Useful for Role Play Practice* ☐

CLOSURES

II: Relaxation

5: Atmosphere

A most helpful element in the closure phase of a session is often a short piece of relaxation work. The leader may invite the group to sit in pairs, back to back, resting their chins on their knees. The leader then describes an alternative environment from the scene which has been role played. This may contain some traditionally relaxing elements such as sun, sand, gentle waves etc.

NB: If this is dramatically different from the atmosphere of the previous exercise, the transition should be as gradual as possible. After relaxing for a short period the group should be encouraged to 'leave behind' that soothing scene and return to the here and now.

Key	
Focus	*Creativity* ☑ *Skills* ☑ *Insight* ☑
Grouping	*Whole Group* ☑ *2* ☑ *3* ☐ *4* ☐ *5* ☐
Time	*5-10 min* ☐ *10-15 min* ☐ *15-20 min* ☐
Anxiety	*Low* ☑ *Medium* ☐ *High* ☐
Music	*Helpful* ☑ *Not relevant* ☐
R.P.P.	*Useful for Role Play Practice* ☐

CLOSURES

II: Relaxation

6: Finale

A variation on the relaxation exercise is to invite people to sit in pairs, back to back, with eyes closed. Members should imagine they have just been in a theatre watching a play in which they have *also* participated. The play is not ended but has come to a temporary pause. Visualise the tableau at the end of the play, with the curtain slowly falling. Gradually, the lights come up and participants find themselves back in the here and now.

They open their eyes and stretch to mark the end of the exercise.

Key	
Focus	*Creativity* ☑ *Skills* ☐ *Insight* ☑
Grouping	*Whole Group* ☑ *2* ☐ *3* ☐ *4* ☐ *5* ☐
Time	*5-10 min* ☑ *10-15 min* ☐ *15-20 min* ☐
Anxiety	*Low* ☑ *Medium* ☐ *High* ☐
Music	*Helpful* ☐ *Not relevant* ☑
R.P.P.	*Useful for Role Play Practice* ☐

CLOSURES

II: Relaxation

7: Candles

The leader instructs the group to stand quite still and leave behind all the work they have been doing. They gently close their eyes and imagine that each is a lighted candle which slowly begins to melt. As the candles gradually melt the group gently sinks to the floor.

NB: Members will probably require being talked through this exercise by slow degrees.

The aim of this activity is to arrive, finally, full length and quite relaxed on the floor but with the flame of the candle still alight inside the person's head. Finally, members stretch, open their eyes and sit up.

Key	
Focus	*Creativity* ☑ *Skills* ☑ *Insight* ☑
Grouping	*Whole Group* ☑ *2* ☐ *3* ☐ *4* ☐ *5* ☐
Time	*5-10 min* ☐ *10-15 min* ☐ *15-20 min* ☑
Anxiety	*Low* ☑ *Medium* ☑ *High* ☐
Music	*Helpful* ☐ *Not relevant* ☑
R.P.P.	*Useful for Role Play Practice* ☐

CLOSURES

II: Relaxation

8: Recapitulation

Members lie down on the floor in their most comfortable position, stretch their bodies to the limits, and then make themselves comfortable again, concentrating particularly on tension in the back of the neck, the spine and the chest.

The leader then asks them to picture the group session in their mind's eye and to remember all the different things that have happened, picturing them rather as if a video were being played. Any moments or incidents which were not fully understood should be noted, but the 'video' should be allowed to run through to the end and be finally switched off.

Members should then feel free to start thinking about waking up, stretching, yawning, and finally sitting up.

Key	
Focus	*Creativity* ☑ *Skills* ☐ *Insight* ☑
Grouping	*Whole Group* ☑ *2* ☐ *3* ☐ *4* ☐ *5* ☐
Time	*5-10 min* ☑ *10-15 min* ☐ *15-20 min* ☐
Anxiety	*Low* ☑ *Medium* ☐ *High* ☐
Music	*Helpful* ☐ *Not relevant* ☑
R.P.P.	*Useful for Role Play Practice* ☐

CLOSURES

III: Guided Focus

9: Integration

For this exercise, the whole group stands in a circle holding
hands. Members close their eyes and think back to how they felt
when they arrived at the group.

They should also trace in their minds the aspects they liked
and those they did not like; the things that puzzled them; and
the points they feel inclined to take away from the group and
give further thought to. There should be at least one important
thing to take away.

Each individual should bring his thoughts right up to the here
and now — to the end of the group session — open his eyes and
look at each person in the circle.

Key	
Focus	*Creativity* ☐ *Skills* ☐ *Insight* ☑
Grouping	*Whole Group* ☑ *2* ☐ *3* ☐ *4* ☐ *5* ☐
Time	*5-10 min* ☐ *10-15 min* ☑ *15-20 min* ☐
Anxiety	*Low* ☐ *Medium* ☑ *High* ☑
Music	*Helpful* ☐ *Not relevant* ☑
R.P.P.	*Useful for Role Play Practice* ☐

III: Guided Focus

10: Reacknowledging the Group

For this closure activity, the group hold hands in a circle, glance quickly around the circle to remind themselves who is there, and then close their eyes.

One by one, each group member should be pictured in the mind's eye. Where are they standing? What are they wearing? Who is standing on either side of them? Who is standing on either side of you?

Still in silence, members can open their eyes and check how accurate they were.

The object of this exercise is for members to 'see' and acknowledge the presence of everyone else in the room.

Key	
Focus	*Creativity* ☑ *Skills* ☐ *Insight* ☑
Grouping	*Whole Group* ☑ *2* ☐ *3* ☐ *4* ☐ *5* ☐
Time	*5-10 min* ☑ *10-15 min* ☐ *15-20 min* ☐
Anxiety	*Low* ☑ *Medium* ☐ *High* ☐
Music	*Helpful* ☐ *Not relevant* ☑
R.P.P.	*Useful for Role Play Practice* ☐

III: Guided Focus

11: What Am I Taking Away?

Again, for this exercise, the group stands in a circle holding hands with their eyes closed.

The leader explains that the object is to reflect individually on everything that has happened in the group during the session, and to choose one particular thing that has been learnt in the group: something which to the individual has felt important and worth taking away to think about.

Members then open their eyes and verbalize what each has chosen, eg. "I am taking away that I *have* got some courage, though I didn't know it before."

Key	
Focus	*Creativity* ☐ *Skills* ☐ *Insight* ☑
Grouping	*Whole Group* ☑ *2* ☐ *3* ☐ *4* ☐ *5* ☐
Time	*5-10 min* ☑ *10-15 min* ☐ *15-20 min* ☐
Anxiety	*Low* ☐ *Medium* ☑ *High* ☐
Music	*Helpful* ☐ *Not relevant* ☑
R.P.P.	*Useful for Role Play Practice* ☐

CLOSURES

IV: Feedback

12: Structured

The leader can obtain feedback from group members in a structured way by asking for 'statements', eg. How did everyone feel at the beginning of the session?

NB: What feeling does everyone have now? Some members may only wish to say a few words, and these may not be very specific, but neither the leader nor other group members should attempt to *analyse* these responses.

The leader, too, can usefully give some feedback to the group. But this should not be judgmental. The differences and similarities in how members have experienced the group can be *noted* but not evaluated.

Key	
Focus	*Creativity* ☐ *Skills* ☑ *Insight* ☑
Grouping	*Whole Group* ☑ *2* ☐ *3* ☐ *4* ☐ *5* ☐
Time	*5-10 min* ☐ *10-15 min* ☑ *15-20 min* ☐
Anxiety	*Low* ☑ *Medium* ☐ *High* ☐
Music	*Helpful* ☐ *Not relevant* ☑
R.P.P.	*Useful for Role Play Practice* ☐

CLOSURES

IV: Feedback

13: Unstructured

If the leader judges it more appropriate to obtain unstructured feedback from the group, it is important to be watchful that the activity is not dominated by one or two more verbal people.

If the latter can be avoided, then it can be extremely fruitful to give the final quarter of the group's time over to an unstructured session in which members may say what they want, using the 'first person'. Only *statements*, and not questions, may be contributed, and members should be encouraged into a *reflective* mood.

The object of this activity is to foster in each individual some thoughtful consideration of how they themselves interacted, felt and performed in the group setting — noting the things they felt important or found unclear.

NB: The leader should be watchful for any member who may be inclined to destroy what everyone else has achieved by simply dismissing it as insignificant.

Key	
Focus	*Creativity* ☑ *Skills* ☑ *Insight* ☑
Grouping	*Whole Group* ☑ *2* ☐ *3* ☐ *4* ☐ *5* ☐
Time	*5-10 min* ☐ *10-15 min* ☑ *15-20 min* ☑
Anxiety	*Low* ☑ *Medium* ☑ *High* ☐
Music	*Helpful* ☐ *Not relevant* ☑
R.P.P.	*Useful for Role Play Practice* ☐

CLOSURES

IV: Feedback

14: Symbolic

For this activity, small cards and felt tip pens are required. The group sits in a circle.

First, the leader should allow a brief transition from the development phase of the session in order to check out any important verbal feedback.

Members are then asked to look at the person sitting next to them on their right, and to imagine what gift they would like to give that person 'to help them on their journey'.

This gift could be a specific object such as a flower or a puppy, or it may perhaps be a quality such as tenacity.

The gifts should be written on card (with a little illustration drawn if possible) and handed to neighbours simultaneously.

Key	
Focus	*Creativity* ☐ *Skills* ☐ *Insight* ☑
Grouping	*Whole Group* ☑ *2* ☐ *3* ☐ *4* ☐ *5* ☐
Time	*5-10 min* ☑ *10-15 min* ☐ *15-20 min* ☐
Anxiety	*Low* ☑ *Medium* ☐ *High* ☐
Music	*Helpful* ☐ *Not relevant* ☑
R.P.P.	*Useful for Role Play Practice* ☐

V: Movement

15: Circles

It is advisable for the leader to work out this dance movement routine with friends or colleagues before introducing it to the group. It should be built up *stage by stage*, and then put together.

Members are invited to move around the room, opening their arms, filling their lungs, and stretching right through to their fingertips.

They should then move *with two or three others* around the room, in a circle, still with arms outstretched and following the person in front. After a while, members should turn and walk in the opposite direction, so they each have a different person to follow. After this, the group could turn inwards to face into the circle, hold hands and move round in a circle one way and then the other.

Finally, individuals can leave the small circle and move in circles around the room, eventually forming a large circle with the whole group and moving around with arms outstretched.

The precise groupings and movements can be planned by the leader.

Key	
Focus	*Creativity* ☑ *Skills* ☑ *Insight* ☑
Grouping	*Whole Group* ☑ *2* ☐ *3* ☑ *4* ☑ *5* ☐
Time	*5-10 min* ☑ *10-15 min* ☐ *15-20 min* ☐
Anxiety	*Low* ☑ *Medium* ☐ *High* ☐
Music	*Helpful* ☑ *Not relevant* ☐
R.P.P.	*Useful for Role Play Practice* ☐

V: Movement

16: Improvisation

For this activity, everyone finds a space, closes their eyes and focuses on their feelings of that moment.

Members then open their eyes and move to the music, attempting to express any left-over feelings through movement rather than in words.

Movements may at first be exaggerated but should be modified and softened gradually, so the exercise finishes in a more relaxed mode.

NB: It is important that the leader allows sufficient time for members to return to their ordinary rhythms before bringing the exercise to a close.

Key	
Focus	*Creativity* ☑ *Skills* ☑ *Insight* ☑
Grouping	*Whole Group* ☑ *2* ☐ *3* ☐ *4* ☐ *5* ☐
Time	*5-10 min* ☑ *10-15 min* ☐ *15-20 min* ☐
Anxiety	*Low* ☑ *Medium* ☐ *High* ☐
Music	*Helpful* ☑ *Not relevant* ☐
R.P.P.	*Useful for Role Play Practice* ☐

CLOSURES

V: Movement

17: Structured

For this exercise, group members stand in a circle with their eyes closed.

The leader talks the group through a sequence of movements during which they can experience alternate tension and relaxation, eg. tense your knees . . . and now let them relax.

Instructions may be given systematically, starting from the top of the body and working down to the feet.

Check out specific tension spots, eg. back of neck, bottom of spine, tight shoulders, tense knuckles, furrowed brows.

To conclude the exercise, members should stretch, yawn widely, and open their eyes. The leader then checks that everyone feels ready to leave the session.

Key	
Focus	*Creativity* ☑ *Skills* ☐ *Insight* ☑
Grouping	*Whole Group* ☑ *2* ☐ *3* ☐ *4* ☐ *5* ☐
Time	*5-10 min* ☑ *10-15 min* ☑ *15-20 min* ☐
Anxiety	*Low* ☑ *Medium* ☐ *High* ☐
Music	*Helpful* ☑ *Not relevant* ☐
R.P.P.	*Useful for Role Play Practice* ☐

CLOSURES

V: Movement

18: Massage

Before introducing this activity, it is important that the leader checks that people are not anxious about *touch*.

Members stand behind their partner, and use their thumbs to relax the shoulders and the back of the neck. With the heel of the hand, they can also rub down the spine in little circles, then with the flat of both hands, rub over the whole of the back.

If the group is likely to treat the following seriously, and not get silly, members can finally use tiny karate 'chopping' movements with both hands up and down the back of their partners' legs.

The partners then change places so the other person can 'be relaxed'.

Key	
Focus	*Creativity* ☑ *Skills* ☐ *Insight* ☑
Grouping	*Whole Group* ☑ *2* ☑ *3* ☐ *4* ☐ *5* ☐
Time	*5-10 min* ☑ *10-15 min* ☐ *15-20 min* ☐
Anxiety	*Low* ☑ *Medium* ☑ *High* ☐
Music	*Helpful* ☐ *Not relevant* ☑
R.P.P.	*Useful for Role Play Practice* ☐

V: Movement

19: Game

For this exercise, members stand in a circle, close enough to be able to massage the neck of the person to their right without stretching. They may also massage the neck, 'Karate chop' the legs, blow a 'hot potato' through their shirts, even smack their bottoms, and then — so long as they are close enough together — sit on the knees of the person behind.

Then everyone stands up and turns a half circle so that they have a *different* person in front of them to work on.

This game usually combines physical relaxation with a reduction of tension through laughter.

Key	
Focus	*Creativity* ☑ *Skills* ☑ *Insight* ☐
Grouping	*Whole Group* ☑ *2* ☐ *3* ☐ *4* ☐ *5* ☐
Time	*5-10 min* ☑ *10-15 min* ☐ *15-20 min* ☐
Anxiety	*Low* ☑ *Medium* ☑ *High* ☐
Music	*Helpful* ☐ *Not relevant* ☑
R.P.P.	*Useful for Role Play Practice* ☐

CLOSURES

VI: Diaries

20: Private Feelings

For this exercise, felt tip pens and paper, or a special diary book, are required. This activity should be timed very precisely.

Members spend 5 minutes 'free writing' about how they are feeling at the end of the group session. This 'diary' is not to be shared with any other member of the group, or with the leader. It is purely personal.

If anyone feels unable to write because they have a 'block' about what to say, then they should be encouraged to write a little about being stuck.

Key	
Focus	*Creativity* ☑ *Skills* ☐ *Insight* ☑
Grouping	*Whole Group* ☑ *2* ☐ *3* ☐ *4* ☐ *5* ☐
Time	*5-10 min* ☑ *10-15 min* ☐ *15-20 min* ☐
Anxiety	*Low* ☑ *Medium* ☐ *High* ☐
Music	*Helpful* ☐ *Not relevant* ☑
R.P.P.	*Useful for Role Play Practice* ☐

CLOSURES

VI: Diaries

21: Influential People

Again, felt pens, paper or a special diary book are required.

Members are asked to think about someone very important in their life *now*, and then spend no more that 5 minutes writing *as if they were* that important person watching the progress of this group.

Individuals finally tell the group who they have selected, and why they are important; but they should *not* share with the group what that person has said. The writing is a private activity to be thought about alone.

Key	
Focus	*Creativity* ☐ *Skills* ☐ *Insight* ☑
Grouping	*Whole Group* ☑ *2* ☐ *3* ☐ *4* ☐ *5* ☐
Time	*5-10 min* ☑ *10-15 min* ☐ *15-20 min* ☐
Anxiety	*Low* ☐ *Medium* ☑ *High* ☑
Music	*Helpful* ☐ *Not relevant* ☑
R.P.P.	*Useful for Role Play Practice* ☐

CLOSURES

VI: Diaries

22: A Private Letter

For this exercise, felt tip pens and paper are required.

Each member thinks of someone important in their life at the present: someone with whom they would like to share something special, perhaps about the group.

They write a letter to that person, describing what the individual has been doing in the group and how it feels.

Finally, members may share with the whole group *who* they have chosen and why they are important, and even how it feels to write to them. But they should *not* divulge what is in the letter, which remains private.

Key	
Focus	*Creativity* ☐ *Skills* ☑ *Insight* ☑
Grouping	*Whole Group* ☑ *2* ☐ *3* ☐ *4* ☐ *5* ☐
Time	*5-10 min* ☑ *10-15 min* ☐ *15-20 min* ☐
Anxiety	*Low* ☑ *Medium* ☑ *High* ☐
Music	*Helpful* ☐ *Not relevant* ☑
R.P.P.	*Useful for Role Play Practice* ☐

CLOSURES

VII: Ritual

23: Directed

The leader will need to work on this activity before introducing it to the group. Thought must be given to what sort of endings can be expressed through movement, or sound, a special song or a special dance. It is preferable to create something original, but it is quite legitimate to use something one has seen, combining a rhythm, song or movement that the group can easily learn and remember.

The activity should draw to a close *calmly*. The age of members and the nature of the group must be borne in mind. For example, young children would respond well to a clapping song, whilst elderly people might prefer a traditional community song. Movement *and* sound should be combined where possible, and musical instruments may also be introduced if appropriate.

Key	
Focus	*Creativity* ☑ *Skills* ☐ *Insight* ☑
Grouping	*Whole Group* ☑ *2* ☐ *3* ☐ *4* ☐ *5* ☐
Time	*5-10 min* ☐ *10-15 min* ☑ *15-20 min* ☐
Anxiety	*Low* ☑ *Medium* ☐ *High* ☐
Music	*Helpful* ☑ *Not relevant* ☐
R.P.P.	*Useful for Role Play Practice* ☐

VII: Ritual

24: Group-evolved

This activity is appropriate for a group with whom the leader has worked for some time. The object is for group members themselves, having covered a range of shared experiences, to find a way of closing the session.

The leader asks members to evolve an appropriate way of ending, perhaps using something they have already done, eg. they might choose to elaborate on a movement exercise.

If they would like music, they should choose what type would suit their own evolved ritual. This may be some music or rhythm they have already encountered in the group sessions, or it may equally be from somewhere else.

NB: Members should be encouraged to arrive at a concensus, taking into account *all* contributions and ideas, within reason!

Key	
Focus	*Creativity* ☑ *Skills* ☐ *Insight* ☑
Grouping	*Whole Group* ☑ *2* ☐ *3* ☐ *4* ☐ *5* ☐
Time	*5-10 min* ☐ *10-15 min* ☐ *15-20 min* ☑ ☐
Anxiety	*Low* ☑ *Medium* ☑ *High* ☐
Music	*Helpful* ☑ *Not relevant* ☐
R.P.P.	*Useful for Role Play Practice* ☐

CLOSURES

VII: Ritual

25: Group Movement

For this activity, a familiar, rhythmic piece of music is selected. The group can be asked to clap the rhythm and familiarize themselves with the tune etc.

The first phrase of the music should be isolated, and the rhythm repeated four times, with an appropriate movement sequence created by the group leader and followed by the rest of the group.

Then each member creates a simple movement sequence to that same rhythm, for the whole group to follow. The individual sequences can then be combined, so that a long sequence is gradually built up, with frequent repetitions as members 'learn' new contributions.

NB: A movement sequence can be as simple as two slow handclaps, one high and one low, then three quick claps. Or it can be as complex as a dance movement, depending on the capabilities of the group. Nothing *too* adventurous should be attempted.

The final sequence of movements will be special to that group, and could be repeated at the end of every session.

Key	
Focus	*Creativity* ☑ *Skills* ☑ *Insight* ☐
Grouping	*Whole Group* ☑ *2* ☐ *3* ☐ *4* ☐ *5* ☐
Time	*5-10 min* ☐ *10-15 min* ☑ *15-20 min* ☐
Anxiety	*Low* ☑ *Medium* ☐ *High* ☐
Music	*Helpful* ☑ *Not relevant* ☐
R.P.P.	*Useful for Role Play Practice* ☐

Appendix

My Family Now

1. "My family now".

This is a further example of the exercise on page 155 entitled: "II: Spectograms; 13 Animals".

2. "My father used to beat me when he was drunk."

3. "There's always someone else present when I'm in bed . . ."

2 & 3 above are further examples of the Visual Dynamics exercise on page 156 entitled: "II Spectograms; 14 Miniatures".

NOTES

NOTES

NOTES

NOTES